sticky
wisdom

How to Start a Creative Revolution at Work

First published 2002 by
Capstone Publishing Limited (A Wiley Company)
The Atrium
Southern Gate
Chichester
West Sussex
PO19 8SQ
www.wileyeurope.com

Reprinted April 2003, October 2003, January 2004, March 2004, September 2004, October 2004
February 2005, August 2005, December 2005, April 2006, August 2006 , December 2006, July 2007,
January 2008

CIP catalogue records for this book are available from the British Library and the US Library of Congress

ISBN 978-1-84112-021-8 (PB)

Designed and typeset by Baseline, Oxford, UK
Printed and bound by TJ International Ltd
This book is printed on acid-free paper

Substantial discounts on bulk quantities of Capstone books are available to corporations, professional associations and other organisations.

Please contact John Wiley & Sons for more details on (+44)1243-770441 or (fax) (+44)1243-770571 or (e-mail) corporatedevelopement@wiley.co.uk

?WHAT IF!
The Innovation Company

sticky
wisdom

Simple, practical
learning about
creativity that will
stick with you
forever

How to Start a Creative Revolution at Work

CAPSTONE

[what if?]

What if we wrote a book about creative behaviours, not based on theory but on our experiences? What if we wrote a book about these creative behaviours – stuff we know works – that brought together our tried and tested creative tools and a practical wisdom that would stick with you forever?

Daz Rudkin, Dave Allan, Kris Murrin and I did just that in 1999. It was called *?What If!* and subtitled **How to Start a Creative Revolution at Work.**

Sticky Wisdom is a revised and updated version of that book.

Thanks

Special thanks to key contributors: Adrian Simpson, Bernie Evans (for book title), Caroline Cornwell, Chris Brown, Dan Goldstone, Dan Proctor, Emma Johns, Gary Joyce, Helen Clements, Jon Platt, Matt White, Meldrum Duncan, Nina Powell, Peter Walter, Rupert Millington, Sal Pajwani and Simon Byerley.

Love and thanks to the fabulous team at ?What *If!* This book is about your work and is dedicated to you: Adrian Simpson, Alex Wright, Alice Kingdon, Andrew Arrojo, Andrew Duffy, Anne-Marie McDonnell, Anwen Brooks, Bhanita Mistry, Ben Stevens, Bernie Evans, Bob Espey, Bob Sheridan, Boris Alberda, Caroline Cornwell, Caroline Foley, Chloe Peacock, Chris Brown, Christian Eldridge, Dan Goldstone, Dan Proctor, Darren Robinson, Dave Allan, David Cardno, Daz Rudkin, Ed Herten, Elizabeth Lindsay, Emma Johns, Emma-May Morley, Emma Stoddart, Fiona Duffy, Gary Joyce, Gordon Peterson, Helen Clements, Irene O'Riordan, Jackie Naghten,

Jacqueline McSwiney, James Baderman, James Clent, Jim Lusty, Jo Foster, Jon Platt, Julia Hoare, Julianne Vanderkar, Karen Scorey, Kristina Murrin, Lipika Mandal, Lizzie Allan, Lorna MacKinnon, Lucie Everist, Lucy Wills, Maddi Riddell, Marilien Romme, Matt Hart, Matt Kingdon, Matt White, Mathew Burrington, Matthew Spencer, Meldrum Duncan, Nikki Taylor, Nina Powell, Norma McComb, Olivia Wright, Paul Wilson, Peter Walter, Phil Davis, Rizwan Aslam, Rupert Millington, Sally-Ann Watson, Sal Pajwani, Sarah Pajwani, Sean Henderson, Shannon Howes, Simon Byerley, Simon Gardner, Sophie Grenville, Sukh Bhathal, Suz Wall, Suzi Morley, Tim Haywood and Vanessa Mayneris.

Thanks to you all.

Matt Kingdon

Editor

March 2002

The Innovation Company
THE GLASSWORKS
3-4 Ashland Place
LONDON W1U 4AH
UNITED KINGDOM
T +44 (0) 20 7535 7500
F +44 (0) 20 7224 0433
W www.whatifinnovation.com

Please contact us with your comments at:
explorer@whatif.co.uk

[explorer]

Contents

Momentum 109

How does it feel to be working on a project that has momentum? You can feel the positive buzz in the air. We like to think of it as 'unreasonable urgency'. You can spot the energy and excitement a mile off. In this chapter you will learn how to dismantle the barriers to momentum and replace them with passion, alignment and emotional openness.

Signalling 143

Signalling is an 'enabling' behaviour, practised by highly creative people, which alongside courage underpins the first four behaviours, to strengthen and sustain their growth. Here we will help you develop awareness of the two states of business thinking and how to navigate between them. We will explain the use of visual, verbal and physical signals and we'll give you practical and priceless signalling tools for both one-to-one and group situations.

Courage 163

Why is it that we admire courage and bravery so much in others but find it hard to practise it ourselves? Why do brave people never consider themselves brave? What are the barriers to courage and bravery and how can we overcome them? Here you will find the five practical steps to lasting courage and creativity.

A call to arms 183

Index 188

Sticky Wisdom

welcome to the revolution

'Innovation and creativity are vital to our growth.'

9/10 people we talk to strongly agree with this statement.

So do you know how to practise and inspire creativity in your day-to-day life at work?

Ask this question and 9/10 people admit the answer is 'no'.

Why is this?

Doing not talking

Instinctively, we all know creativity at work is important. If creativity sees the commercial light of day, if it actually happens, that's innovation; and innovation means growth. So ultimately all our business futures depend on our ability to be creative at work.

We've been told about the need for innovation – about the need for a creative revolution – for a long time now, and not just in magazines and journals but from Chairmen and CEOs. For shareholders it's music to the ears but what's missing in most cases is the practical follow-through. Companies often talk about why they need innovation but seldom know how they are going to do it.

Why is this? Most people in business accept that innovation and creativity is 'important', but it's rarely classified as 'urgent', because the bottom line benefits of a creative act may not be felt for one, two, even three years. This does not easily fit the often short-term focus of modern business. Moreover, because creativity is seen as 'easy to talk about but hard to do', it can be intimidating; so companies don't bother.

There are other convenient reasons not to engage with creativity. There is always something else potentially more urgent... 'I need to get the core business sorted before I can even think about creativity.' 'If only I could recruit more people.' 'If only I had more funds.' 'I need more time to think.'

All of these reasons make it easy to put creativity on the back burner, something to be addressed later. The problem is there isn't a 'right time'.

If creativity is important to your business, the time to start is **now**.

This book contains what you need to start a creative revolution in your organisation; to get creativity working for you. It aims to demystify creativity at work by going beyond theory, providing a set of practical tools that will help you to just get on with it.

Why be creative?

We use the words creativity and innovation a lot in this book; they are often seen as interchangeable, but to us they mean quite different things. By our definition, creativity only becomes innovation when ideas become useful. In the business world, that means when a new product or service is launched, or starts to make money. Creativity is a behaviour; innovation is a process.

Today, the business case for innovation is almost universally accepted. In recent years, company after company has tried to become more innovative to improve its competitiveness. But we believe it goes deeper than that; creativity is in our blood. It's a skill we all have and can all enjoy, whether it's inventing a new game with your children, painting your kitchen purple or landscaping your garden, we all recognise the joy and pride that comes from having an idea and making it happen. It's our ability to create, to make previously unseen connections, which really defines us as human beings.

Creativity is the greatest and most under developed skill in business today. In America, for example, the Intellectual Property Association has estimated that the so-called creative sectors – chiefly communications, information, entertainment, science and technology – are now far more valuable than automobiles, aerospace or agriculture.

But it's not just software developers and research scientists who require creative skills. Everything from problem-solving to process design, from strategy to customer service, requires creativity. Today, in every industry and at every level, companies are desperate for employees to be more innovative, flexible, imaginative, motivated, open to change. They want them to reinvent their jobs, processes, organisations, working practices, and just about everything else.

Two worlds

Every single one of us can be more creative. Creative behaviour can be learned. The problem is that either we don't feel like bringing our innate creativity to work with us, or the business unwittingly suppresses it.

We believe there are two worlds to business, an **analytical** world and a **creative** world. Most large organisations have both, but they have much too much of the analytical world, leaving less opportunity for creative behaviour to take root and grow.

Our creative revolution doesn't advocate dismantling the traditional world of business – we think that world is fine most of the time. What we're saying is that when creativity is on the menu we need to switch to another more creative world.

Ironically, the more successful companies become, the more they lose touch with their entrepreneurial roots. Over time, they develop systems that end up beating the life out of creativity. They get stuck in the analytical world, and find it harder and harder to step into the creative one. How and why the entrepreneurial spirit dies with corporate growth is an important issue, and one that we will explore further in this book.

Failure to navigate between the traditional world of 'analysis' and the world of 'creativity' not only compromises business growth, it undermines personal growth and job satisfaction, reducing feelings of fulfilment through work. Shutting off creative behaviour denies ourselves part of who we are. Yes, we all come to work to earn money, but there is much more to our motivations than that.

Why listen to us?

?What *If!* is an innovation company based in London, UK. Our mission is to help large companies and organisations that have become stale recapture their inventive spirit and so make work a fantastic part of their people's lives.

One hundred passionate individuals work at ?What *If!* and, since we started in 1992, we've been lucky enough to help shape the culture of some of the world's biggest, fastest growing, and most profitable organisations. We have helped our clients invent new airports, beers, stores, toys, holidays, shampoos and mortgages.

In that time, we have led hundreds of innovation projects and trained more than 6000 people all over the world in creative behaviours. We have also developed tools and techniques to kick-start enduring creative cultures in commercial and government organisations. Our intention has been to set up a unique way of working we call an 'inside-out culture'. Part of that culture is to try new things habitually. We have had some spectacular disasters and phenomenal successes. As a result we have built up a vast store-cupboard of practical knowledge about how innovation really works, and what prevents it happening.

Constant experimentation allows us to keep pushing creativity deeper into the hearts of our clients' organisations as well as our own. In our business, you can forget theories. You can only teach creativity by doing creativity. Everything we learn about designing and running innovation projects feeds into what we teach in our creativity workshops.

The other aspect of an 'inside-out culture' is that we try very hard to be what we teach. We have directly experienced all of the creative behaviours described in this book. Our battle-cry is 'Living Innovation' and when we do live these behaviours we know that they work. We have seen the results when we introduce them to clients and when we practise them ourselves.

Why behaviours?

This book is about behaviours, being different, and trying new and different things. Unlike most business books, our challenge is not just to change the way you think, it's to change the way you act. We have found that focusing on behaviours is the most effective way of inspiring creative change.

Implementing and adopting new behaviours affects the way you feel. Maybe not instantly, but after a while you will definitely feel your creative capacity increase. Believe us, this stuff really works! If you've ever been out for the evening feeling low, but decided to put a smile on your face anyway, you will know what we mean. In a short time your mood changes, your smile makes you feel more positive. Creative behaviour works in the same way. Behave creatively and you will feel creative.

So what do creative people do that's different?

At present, many people think creativity is the preserve of a certain type of person. Just telling people to be more creative doesn't help. So we have deliberately broken creativity down into six separate behaviours to make it accessible to everyone. Once you look at it in this simple way, creativity falls off its pedestal; it becomes like any other sort of activity, easy to talk about, practise and measure. Creativity is something we can all get on and do.

Our creative revolution involves adopting six specific behaviours, which we call freshness, greenhousing, realness, momentum, signalling and courage.

A survey we carried out of 500 middle managers from large multinationals, and 500 inventors (people who have patented at least one idea and get a significant proportion of their income from their own inventions) showed inventors were significantly more likely to exhibit the six behaviours than their managerial counterparts. The specific behaviours where inventors exhibited the greatest difference from managers were: greenhousing (15% more), realness (21% more) and courage (17% more).

These results probably won't surprise you. We all know that creative people spend their time in slightly different ways and, as we examine each of the six behaviours, we are sure many of our observations will resonate for you. That's because they tap into intuitive knowledge that you already possess. Whatever your job, whatever you do, the principles in this book can be adapted and applied to how you work.

But in the end, the value you extract will be in direct proportion to your willingness to take a leap and try out some of these behaviours – it's really up to you. However, the fact you are reading this book suggests you are already open to a new way of working, one that releases your creative potential.

In this book we have collected all the experience and practical wisdom we have about encouraging creativity at work and written it down in a simple, no bullshit, style. That's because we want you to remember it and give it a go.

We want the wisdom to stick. Welcome to the revolution.

freshness

In a world where business is more interested in 'best practice' rather than different practise, is it any wonder that products and services, companies and organisations are all beginning to look the same?

Is this you?

- ◆ You do the same things every day. Take the same route to work, read the same newspaper and listen to the same radio station in the morning.

- ◆ You spend most of your time with people from similar backgrounds.

- ◆ You rarely go out of your way to try new things, meet new people or go to new places

- ◆ You're so busy that you settle for the first good solution to a problem.

- ◆ You suspect many of your ideas could easily be copied by your competitors.

- ◆ If you were really honest with yourself, you'd agree your ideas were more incremental than revolutionary.

Why freshness matters

Next time you finish a brainstorm, or put the final touches to your annual plan, step back and pause to look at the ideas you've generated. If you were being completely honest, how many of those ideas do you think your competitors could also come up with? Our experience tells us that many organisations don't ask themselves this question because of the awesome implications of their answer. Shocking, isn't it, when we are relying on these very ideas to deliver growth in a competitive environment?

Part of the problem is that most of us are so wrapped up in a busy work schedule we seldom make time to question the quality and uniqueness of our ideas. Sometimes we are just so thankful to have a plan or agreement within our organisation, that we don't want to upset the apple cart by asking difficult questions about whether our competitors have the same plan. The truth is that competitive organisations are not always as competitive as they'd like to think they are. For a start, they often draw on a remarkably similar skill base, employing the same kind of people from the same backgrounds. What's more, they access and use similar data, and talk to the same consumers in the same way. They get excited when they spot a 'new' insight, apparently unaware that nine times out of ten competitors will be looking at the same information and getting excited about the very same insight!

You can see this in almost any category of product or service; companies launching similar initiatives at the same time in the same way. So much of what is expected to be step-change innovation is little more than another ride on the merry-go-round of incrementalism.

There is a very simple law in operation here, the first law of creativity – the quality and uniqueness of *stimulus in* has a direct impact on the quality and uniqueness of *ideas out.*

This is the basis of freshness, and it's why creative people and organisations do not rely on the same data their competitors have access to. They source a wider diet, seeking out new experiences and ways of thinking about their market, products and internal processes. This provides the critical stimulus that allows them to see and think about issues in a different way. The new perspectives they gain provoke them into making creative connections that others won't have made.

"Go where your competitors can't or won't."

ANITA RODDICK, FOUNDER OF THE BODY SHOP

What is stimulus?

Stimulus is any experience that is new to you or outside the boundaries of the problem you are dealing with. This is important. Stimulus is not a new idea in itself but the raw material of the creative process. In our experience, if you've got good stimuli, you won't be able to stop yourself from being creative – the unique connections will just flow from that.

Some people are highly disciplined about taking in fresh new experiences. They deliberately organise experiences for themselves and their teams. For others the process is more intuitive. Their raw material for creativity is constantly topped up by a deep curiosity about the world. Whether by design or instinct, the most creative people and organisations ensure they get a bit of each. Freshness can be both a personal and corporate behaviour, which secures genuine competitive advantage, because 'true' freshness is impossible to replicate.

The behaviour of freshness is the continual search for different experiences that jolt you into making new and unique connections. Whilst creativity may appear entirely intuitive, it is in fact a skill you can develop, practise and plan into your everyday life. This chapter will show you how.

It will explore why stimulus is the key to creativity and how you can inject freshness into your everyday working life. We will introduce the concept of 'river-jumping' (using techniques to stimulate fresh thinking at any time), and then look at the long-term behaviour changes necessary to build up your 'freshness store-cupboard'.

"New ideas come from differences. They come from having different perspectives and juxtaposing different theories."

NICHOLAS NEGROPONTE, AUTHOR

But first, let us take you on a brief journey to explore the workings of that most amazing human organ, the brain. We'll tell you why it's hard-wired to make creativity difficult and how to use stimulus to trick it out of its non-creative channel.

The world's greatest filing system

The human brain is an amazing piece of equipment that unfortunately hasn't come with a user's manual. Since the late 1950s a huge amount has been learnt about its structure and abilities, yet few people have been taught how to maximise its potential. However, it has been discovered that the brain's main default setting actively inhibits the ability to think creatively. Unless you learn how to work around this, your potential to produce new ideas will be severely limited.

The brain has a function known as a 'self-organising mechanism'. It automatically sorts all the data it takes in without your having to think about it. Like a huge filing system, information is digested and stored in a logical and easily retrievable way. The brain classifies and interprets new information by looking for similarities with what's already on file. So when you see something new, your brain will automatically ask, 'Where have I seen something like this before?' and it goes into its filing system to look for it. When it finds what it's looking for it opens that existing file and uses the memories stored there as a point of reference to generate thoughts and make decisions. You can see this in the exercise below.

TRY THIS

What sort of car does each of these people drive?

Because you don't personally know these people you've had to guess. Your brain's automatic response is to jump into a 'river of thinking' based on previous experiences. Perhaps you 'guessed' the man in the suit drove a Lexus, the woman a hatchback and the man in the open-neck shirt a BMW? Whatever you guessed is not important for this exercise, it's *how* you did it that's important. The connections you made were based on past experience – it was the brain's filing system at work.

As we have seen, faced with any situation, the brain's automatic response is to put us into a 'river of thinking' based on previous experiences. If you want to test this, next time you go on a long car journey, play this simple game. When you pass a car take a glance at the driver and passengers, make up a story about who these people are, where they are going and why. It's amazingly easy to do. From just that quick glance at the make of car, the ages and dress of the occupants and other details, a whole life for these people can be imagined. This is the brain's filing system at work.

Human beings have the capacity to take in huge amounts of information. The sheer volume of data we absorb means it would be virtually impossible for us to work out and interpret everything from the word 'go'. Instead we make educated guesses based on similarities and past experience. The brain simply says, 'I don't really need to know, from first principles, how to act, respond or judge a certain situation every time I see it. What I'll do instead is direct you, based on what I've seen before that looks similar.'

Imagine if this process were visual; that information were like rain falling on a hillside. The brain would decide which river to funnel the rainwater down by looking for similarities with past experiences. The more the rainwater fell, the more the brain would connect the similarities and the deeper the rivers would become. Imagine how paralysing life would be if the brain didn't act in this way, if every day you had to find out how and where to put your socks on. Instead the brain simply says, 'that looks like a sock, it'll go on your foot.'

This basic brain classification system has been developing and growing since you were born. An infant's brain is bombarded with millions of new pieces of information which fall like raindrops. The brain starts classifying, creating streams of recognition, which speeds up the sorting process, allowing it to handle more information.

The process continues at school. Over time, you get faster at classifying information by recognition and the rivers become deeper. With good teaching, you continue to add new rivers to the existing ones as different and stimulating ideas come along which challenge your preconceptions. Then you leave school or college and go to work. When the initial excitement of learning about this new environment wears off, the flow of new ideas starts to slow down. But the flow of information speeds up and the rivers have to handle more rain and so they get deeper.

The brain's classification system has huge advantages, allowing people to handle vast amounts of data. But there are two big drawbacks to making such rapid classifications. First, the assumptions the brain makes can sometimes be wrong, causing you to jump to conclusions and make snap decisions about people and situations.

Second, the way the brain processes information kills creativity. Every time you try to think of something new, the brain keeps bringing you back to the original river. It leads you to a 'this is how it is', rather than a 'this is how it could be', scenario. So how can you break away from this? The answer is to deliberately find a way of overriding the brain's classification system. To trick the brain into believing you are thinking about another river, you must get out of the original river altogether, then approach it again from a new and different perspective. This is called a lateral step – we call it 'river-jumping'.

Let's look at an example of how this works.

Imagine you're trying to improve photocopiers and you decide to begin by using an insight based on customer research. This insight is that people find the machines have an annoying habit of getting jammed, or blocked, at critical moments. The company that solves the problem will have a competitive advantage. What's needed is a flash of creativity. But because of the way the brain works every time you try to think about new and different improvements to photocopiers, it pulls you back to the river of current realities and past experiences it has already created. You can't help thinking about how you've tried to sort out this problem before. To generate new ideas you have to use techniques that enable the brain to make new connections. This is where river-jumping comes in. By using a piece of stimulus, we can focus the brain on something completely different, and break out of our 'river of thinking'.

This is how it works. The problem with photocopiers is that they can get blocked. So first of all, and this is important, forget photocopiers altogether. Use a piece of stimulus to look at the issue from a fresh perspective. Your stimulus is to ask the question, 'What else gets blocked?'

Say we come up with 'noses'; noses get blocked when you have a cold. Start to think more about noses. What happens next is that the brain instantly forgets all its rules and past experiences of photocopiers and starts reminding you of the things that relate to noses – a different river altogether.

You've made a lateral step. Now from this very different place turn round and make a connection back to the original topic. In other words, use the nose as a piece of stimulus to think differently about photocopiers. What happens when your nose is blocked? Well, one of the great things about noses is that even when you have a cold both nostrils rarely get blocked at the same time. Now refer back to the original problem. What if photocopiers had a second feed system so that when they got blocked or ran out of toner you just flicked a switch and a second system kicked in? This would relieve the end-users' frustration when the machine jams at a bad moment. Now, thanks to the stimulus, we have an idea that's worth building on. Ideas rarely emerge fully formed, and often need to be built by several rounds of creative iteration – but more on this later.

> **"Problems cannot be solved by thinking within the framework in which they were created."**
> ALBERT EINSTEIN

Remember the stimulus doesn't give the answer; stimulus is not an idea itself, it simply provides fresh context and perspective. Stimulus allows you to jump out of one river of thinking into another; from this new river you can get insights and make new connections back to the first river. And guess what? Now it's much more difficult for your competitors to follow you and make the same connection. In fact, the more rivers you jump in the creative act, the harder it becomes to follow.

Greg Garrison's flight of fancy

In 1993, Greg Garrison was put in charge of a key initiative at the financial services and information giant, Reuters. Garrison was given the task of improving the usability of the computer trading systems the company supplies to the dealing rooms of banks in over 130 countries.

A key aim of new product development was to ensure .that computer systems – especially the graphical interface that the customer sees – can be mastered quickly, so that dealers minimise their down-time. In a business where millions of dollars can be made and lost at the stroke of a keyboard, users of the Reuters systems were understandably reluctant to spend time retraining. Usability was vital. They said they didn't have time to read instruction manuals, but were adept at feeling their way.

What was needed, the Reuters team realised, was a graphical interface that was easy to learn, and could master updated features. With the launch of the company's new product range approaching, the team sought inspiration. But in the pressure cooker atmosphere of the company's London base, the creative juices didn't seem to be flowing. Even the cool-headed Garrison was starting to worry. A breakthrough was needed. But it wasn't going to happen in the office.

Garrison set off on one of his frequent fact-finding missions, travelling to the Far East to talk to customers in other markets. Away from the hustle and bustle of the Fleet Street office, he relaxed. His curiosity returned. He began to search out fresh stimulus to jolt his thinking around the task.

On his return flight he asked to see the flight deck of the 747 he was travelling on. Surrounded by a wall of sophisticated instrumentation, he was amazed at how pilots could move from one aircraft to another in the same class with such ease and without retraining. When he asked them, the pilots explained that instruments were arranged in a logical and consistent way across the 747 class, which made flying one aircraft much the same as any other.

Garrison made a new connection. What if the graphical interface on the next generation of Reuters systems was modelled on a pilot's cockpit? It would mean that switching from one system to an updated system would be relatively straightforward. Back in London, he reported his idea to the rest of the team. The idea took off.

Team members built on the original insight, adding a range of features that included autopilots and navigators, which would help the dealers find their way around the new system. Like a pilot's instrument panel, the idea was to place technical support and training at the customer's fingertips. At the touch of a button, traders would be able to move from the realtime market environment into on-screen simulations, calling up features such as autopilot tools to steer them through products – without having to call Reuters for support. In the end, the system was not implemented in full as it was superseded by adherence to the new Microsoft Office style desktop environment. Nevertheless, many of the tools the aviation metaphor gave rise to were included in the next generation of Reuters products, providing trading and operating support for end-users.

All because Greg Garrison looked outside the environment of his problem and gave himself the stimulus to make a fresh connection – that's the essence of freshness.

Learning how to do river-jumping

So how do you get started? What can you do now to get freshness into your thinking? It is often assumed that creativity is a spontaneous activity, but creative people in the know use tools and techniques to push their thinking. Far from being spontaneous, they plan creative sessions in advance.

As we have seen, understanding the brain's natural classification system is the first step to managing creativity. The ability to make new connections is limited only by the ability to jump out of one river of thinking and into another. The tool you can use to do this is stimulus. Think of it as an investment. You devote a short amount of time to not thinking specifically about the problem or issue, but investing in the stimulus that will subsequently enable you to make far more, and far richer, connections.

Hundreds of tools have been devised to help people stimulate different thinking, but we believe there are in fact only four main categories of behaviour that jump your thinking, and almost all creativity tools fit into one of these areas. Once you understand the underlying principles, you will be able to invent your own techniques tailored to the exact challenge you are working on at the time. To make them easier to remember, each principle starts with the letter R. We call them **the 4Rs**.

They are:

Re-expression – finding an alternative way of describing or experiencing an issue or problem.

Related worlds – looking at other areas where a similar issue or benefit can be seen. (This is the technique used in the photocopier example above.)

Revolution – identifying and then challenging the rules and assumptions we are using.

Random links – making connections and links between the issue and random items found in the world.

Let's look at each of these in more detail.

First R: **Re-expression**

The way tasks and issues are expressed in business tends to be quite limited. Often we rely on business jargon and descriptors, which send us off down the same old rivers of thought. Simply describing or experiencing the issue in a different way will automatically prompt the mind to approach it from a fresh perspective, because the brain will put the new words into a different river.

You can get started with our three favourite re-expression tools.

1 · Re-express with alternative words

As implied, simply replacing key words in your creative challenge will enable your brain to think in a different way. There are many words you use in your business life which become loaded with a certain meaning. When you hear them, your brain automatically sends you into a well-worn river of past association. Re-expression is a technique which tricks the brain out of this often non-creative assumption-making.

If you look at the loyalty example below, you can see how using many different expressions gives the brain lots of potentially new connection points back to the original problem. Similarly, you may re-express loyalty as a powerful metaphor, for example, 'a marriage' – you could then think of the many different ways loyalty is encouraged in a marriage, e.g. courting, ceremony, public commitment, legality, pain of divorce, and use these fresh perspectives to help you reconnect with your 'loyalty' issue.

Loyalty

We recently worked with a major blue chip business to help it find more creative ways of increasing customers' loyalty. Having asked the obvious questions about what loyalty meant and getting the obvious answers (repeat purchase, greater share of second time buyers, etc.), we set about trying to re-express the challenge.

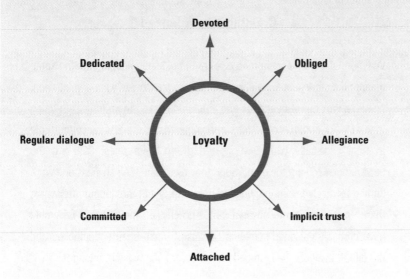

Simply by using alternative words we were able to expand the perception of the problem and open up new avenues of thinking. 'Allegiance' led to an idea about clubs, which consumers paid to join; while 'obliged' led to an idea about a penalty scheme for lack of loyalty.

2 · Re-express using different senses

Using words is only one way to be creative. You have many other senses open to you which you used freely when you were a child, but conceal as an adult – especially as business people. For example, instead of relying on words, why not use a drawing to describe an issue, make a clay model or even act it out to make a physical representation of an issue or a business process. This may all sound a bit weird, but it does work.

Creating a wok legend

We were asked by a large food retailer to help their people 'breathe some life into the stir fry category'. So we got them together in a creative session, 'made' a wok out of beanbags and chairs and asked them to act out being 'a stir fry' for two minutes. Not surprisingly, they were a bit uncomfortable at first, especially when we started giving them roles: 'You are the beansprouts; you are the oil…' Soon they overcame their shyness and were hurling themselves into the wok. All great fun, but at the debrief afterwards there were some acute observations. The chicken thought that he would have probably poisoned someone because he had been undercooked and the oil felt everyone had jumped on her before she was hot enough!

From this session came two key insights about cooking stir fry at home – people cooked at too low a heat; and ingredients went in at the wrong time so were often under or overcooked.

These insights produced two product ideas. First, cooking oil which changed colour when it had reached the right temperature for cooking and second, segmented and numbered packaging which showed the sequence to put the ingredients in and the time they needed to cook properly; the big breakthrough on the second idea was precision-sliced ingredients, cut so they could all go in at the same time.

Bubbling under

Let's look at another re-expression. Here's a picture that was drawn in a creative session.

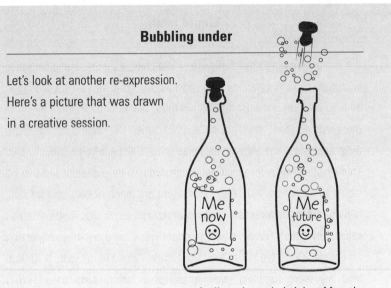

We were exploring how people were feeling about their jobs. After the initial response we asked people to draw their feelings. The person who drew this picture, let's call her Jo, was quiet, but when describing her drawing became animated. 'I feel like the fizzy drink. I feel full of potential but trapped.' Her comments were a rich vein of stimulus that led to many new ideas. Because she re-expressed the issue Jo was able to jump the whole team into a new way of thinking about their jobs. A picture really does say a thousand words!

3 · Re-express from someone else's perspective

Try deliberately describing the world and your issue through the eyes of someone else. For instance, how would an alien describe this? How would your most feared competitor describe it? What about a five-year-old? The creative options are endless.

Liquid teeth

A client once gave us the challenge of launching a toothpaste in countries where the use of toothpaste was very low. The creative session had hit an all time low. The scientist attempting to explain how toothpaste works to the creative team was having a hard time. His molecular structure diagrams were not helping us understand the benefit of the product. Through the glassy-eyed mist we suggested that he explain it to us as he would to a five-year-old. 'Well, kids, teeth are made of calcium,' he said, feeling rather embarrassed. 'And the amazing thing is that toothpaste has calcium in it too!' 'Wow,' said one bright spark, as a creative connection was made. 'Could we talk to the target market about liquid teeth?!' Before long we were tumbling over ourselves to offer ideas based on a toothpaste tube full of liquid teeth – a great creative idea, and all because we tried to re-express our challenge from someone else's perspective.

Second R: **Related worlds**

Never assume that you are the only person to have faced an issue like the one you are facing, or that you cannot learn something valuable from the world around you. 'Related worlds' is a technique that enables you to harness the experiences of others in a creative context. It is the art of identifying situations or events that in some way mirror the creative challenge that you face right now. You probably won't want to steal their ideas or experiences directly, but the principles or stimuli of another's approach can be identified and reapplied to your own challenge.

This is what management writer Tom Peters means when he refers to business people 'swiping with glee'. It is the very opposite of the 'not invented here' syndrome. It means deliberately encouraging people to go out and see what they can learn from others. The creative act occurs when you reapply this to your own challenge in a unique way. The roll-on deodorant is exactly this principle in action. The steal was to look at the ballpoint pen and apply the same principles to deodorant – another world where a liquid had to be spread equally thinly across a surface.

> *"Originality is nothing but judicious imitation."*
> VOLTAIRE

Related worlds is a great principle for demystifying the creative process. All you have to do is ask, 'Where in the world has my challenge (or anything like it) been faced before? What can I learn and steal from that?' Curiously, most people's eyes light up when we re-express creativity as 'stealing'!

To apply the technique start by considering, 'What am I trying to do, or achieve?' Write this as a short summary in the middle of a circle with a set of spokes coming from it. Now invest some time in thinking where else this issue has been encountered. Before long you will have a fabulous wheel of related worlds stimuli to base your creative thinking on.

Making music easier to buy – Virgin Music

As befits their continual focus on the customer, Virgin Music engaged us on a project to help make store layout easier to access for consumers who weren't necessarily music experts. (Virgin had learnt that non-music experts told them it was it hard to find what they wanted in music stores.) We decided to do a related worlds exercise. It looked like this:

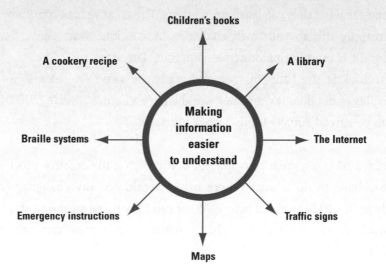

We then spent time investigating each of these worlds – drawing out principles and insights that we could reapply to our own issue. For example, when we looked at maps we realised that they cleverly used lots of symbols to convey complex information. From there we had the idea of creating a symbol for each different sort of music and posting a big visual key right at the front of the store.

Related worlds are everywhere. To start you off try the following.

Other businesses

When was the last time you visited a business outside your category? On a recent project about speed to market, for example, we sought stimulus from McDonald's (an inspiring speed system in action) and Formula 1 cars (pit stops reduced from six minutes to less than 15 seconds in the modern age). We can guarantee another business somewhere sometime has faced a challenge of a similar nature to the one you're working on right now.

Other people with related expertise

We call them 'naive experts' – people expert in your challenge area but not in your business. In a workshop we ran with a food company, our brief was to provide new ways of thinking about health. The brand team – stuck in busy day-to-day jobs – had no way of experiencing fresh perspectives. So over the course of a day we introduced them to eight different 'health experts'. These included the owner of an alternative practise clinic, a gardener, a super-fit 80-year-old, a slob (no interest in health), a personal trainer, a homeopath, a faith-healer and a doctor. Our challenge suddenly felt very new and very broad.

The wider world of science, history or nature

George de Mestral used nature as the stimulus that led to the innovation of Velcro™ after a day of hunting in the Jura mountains in France in 1941. Carefully inspecting the burrs in his woollen clothes and his dog's coat, he found hundreds of little hooks engaging the loops in the material and fur. This natural hook and catch system gave him the initial idea for Velcro™. De Mestral went on to make a machine to duplicate hooks and loops out of nylon.

Third R: **Revolution**

Revolution is creativity at its most provocative. It's the deliberate challenging of the rules and assumptions that exist. Some of the great creative leaps of our time have come from revolution. What if we could fly? What if we could have sex without babies? What if…!

Very often our ability to come up with innovative ideas is limited by the rules that define our particular river. As we saw earlier in this chapter, the mind continually judges ideas and stimuli to try and make them fit with what we know already. Revolution is all about deliberately breaking the mind's rules. So the first step in revolution thinking is to be aware of the rules which already exist in life or in your mind. This can be hard, so deep are the rivers we're in or strong the rules that exist. For instance, nearly all generations of writing implements have copied the original quill shape:

ink pen, pencil and Biro™. It's only recently that pen manufacturers have started to change the rules with inventions like the ball-shaped pen, which actually suits the task of writing better.

When faced with a creative challenge, one of the simple techniques to get you started is to write down the 'rules'. Set as many as you possibly can down on paper. What's the shape, use, feel, touch, application, aesthetics, dimensions, process, etc., etc.? Below is an example from the world of shampoo.

Rules	Revolution
It's liquid	Solid, a mousse, a milk, a cream, etc.
In plastic bottles	Capsules, a beautiful glass bottle, a fabric, etc.
For washing	Cleansing, massage, stimulation, cutting, etc.
Used with water	Dry with your hairdryer, a gas, etc.
Once a day	Morning and night, on the run, at the office, etc.
For beauty	Invigoration, repair, sensitising, pleasure, etc.

You can break each rule in many ways, each of which offers the chance of a fresh perspective or new idea. Once you've got your rules you can start to play around with them. For example, try exaggerating, opposing, reducing, and reversing as many of the assumptions as you can.

FIVE OF OUR FAVOURITE REVOLUTION QUESTIONS ARE:

1 · What if we did nothing?

Rather than getting worried about the difficult-to-pour super-thick consistency of tomato ketchup, Heinz simply turned this feature into a benefit. The advertising campaign leaves a clear message – if it comes out too easily then it must be low-quality ketchup.

2 · What if we had to make it for half the cost?

The humble Mars Bar is a great example of revolution thinking. By filling the centre of chocolate with other, lower-cost sweet ingredients (toffee and caramel), the confectionery market was created and Mars had a worldwide best-seller.

3 · What if people bought twice as much?

What do you get if you double the size of a shopping basket? A basket you can't carry or a basket with wheels. The supermarket trolley was born!

4 · What if we reversed the process?

At the end of the 1980s most car companies were concentrating on big, modern family cars. Two Japanese designers at Mazda reversed this thinking, persuading the company to launch a retro racer based on the Lotus Elan. The MX5 (or Miata as it's known in the US) was launched and the two-seater sports car market reborn.

5 · What if we exaggerated the issue?

The potato chip was invented in 1853 by a Native American, George Crum, who was a chef in a hotel in Saratoga Springs, New York. The story goes that, following guest complaints about George's thick undercooked fries, in a fit of pique he sliced his potatoes as thin as he could and fried them extra long. The guest was delighted and asked for more! Soon the word spread and by 1900 Saratoga Chips were famous over the East Coast of the USA. George Crum would indeed have been surprised that this 'exaggeration' created a $4bn industry in the USA alone!

"Rules are for people who aren't willing to invent their own."

CHUCK YEAGER, FIRST MAN TO BREAK THE SOUND BARRIER

Pollution solution

A few years ago, a city in the Netherlands had a refuse problem. A once clean section of town had become an eyesore because people had stopped using the trashcans. Cigarette butts, beer bottles, chocolate wrappers, newspapers and other trash littered the streets.

Obviously, folk at the sanitation department were concerned, so they sought ways to clean up the city. One idea was to double the littering fine from 25 guilders to 50 guilders for each offence. They tried this, but it had little effect. Then somebody asked the following revolution question:

'What if, instead of punishing the people who drop litter, we reward those who keep the place clean?' At first this seemed daft – how can you reward people who put rubbish in bins?

Fortunately, the people who were listening to this idea didn't evaluate it in the context of current reality. Instead, they just asked in what circumstances it would be possible. In the end, the sanitation department developed electronic trashcans that had a sensing unit on the top that would detect when a piece of refuse had been deposited. This activated a tape recorder that played a recording of a joke. As a result people went out of their way to put their trash in the trashcans, and the town became clean once again.

Fourth R: **Random links**

This is probably the principle that 'feels' the most creative. It is the simple art of selecting at random a piece of stimulus that has *nothing to do with your creative challenge* and then deliberately forcing a connection.

There are only two rules with this technique.

1 · **The random item must be truly random**

You want items which have no connection with what you're working on. The random nature of the stimulus creates surprise and freshness.

2 · **You must find a connection**

The harder you work to find a connection the more likely it is to be unique and therefore interesting. (Remember what we said about competitive advantage.)

For example, imagine you work in telecommunications. Can you force yourself into making a connection between a garden hose system (or lawn sprinkler) and a telephone?

Here goes: what if, like the sprinkler, the telephone had detachable equipment for listening, or you could attach different kinds of equipment to the headset? Or the telephone was made rugged enough for use in any weather conditions? Or what if you set up outdoor electrical points to charge up mobile phones?

The point here is that the stimulus does not give you the idea. Instead it has a whole host of attributes, values and benefits, which you can appropriate and adapt for your challenge. Its value is that it has absolutely nothing to do with your challenge so it will force you to think more broadly – in a way your mind without stimulus may never do.

Putting the 4Rs together

An example brainstorm plan

The great thing about the 4Rs is that they are not prescriptive. They are principles that can be tailored and adapted to any challenge. So when you're sitting at your desk with that 'empty headed… where do I start' feeling, turn to the 4Rs to get you started.

The 4Rs can also be used in a much more formal way as the planning tool for a really good brainstorm session. Here is an example.

Our challenge was to invent breakthrough products for the hair care market. We gathered together a mixed team from sales and marketing, R&D, design and advertising agencies. We also invited some external participants, including consumers and a number of 'naive' experts from other disciplines to keep us fresh. Then for two days we immersed ourselves in a highly stimulated world based on the 4Rs.

Used in this way, they can provide an incredibly powerful framework for creating brainstorms and ideas workshops. No more bare rooms, blank flip charts and blank faces. Instead, an inspired team constantly stimulated with fresh perspectives to provide the basis for genuinely new and different ideas.

Day 1

	ACTIVITY	**PURPOSE**
Day 1 8:30 am	**Kick-start** Facilitators welcome participants, play introductory games, set up the rules of creative behaviour, and explain logistics for the next two days.	Introduce participants. Create welcoming atmosphere. Highlight different ways of working.
9:00 am	**Set-up** Project leader sets up the challenge explaining the purpose of the session in a motivating way.	Participants have a common vision of what success is; they feel valued and motivated.
9:15 am	**First burst** Team gives opening thoughts and ideas they've already had for solving the issue.	People won't have new ideas until they've got their current ideas off their chest.
10:00 am	**Consumer workshop** Live consumer research 'focus' group using appropriate target consumers.	**Re-expression stimulus** Looks at the challenge from the consumer's point of view. Grounds whole session in consumer reality.

Day 1

		ACTIVITY	PURPOSE
1:00 pm		**Act it out** Physically act out the whole hair care process from beginning to end as a piece of hair. (What does it feel like to be dirty/washed/dried/ styled?) Experience acting out each new alternative.	**Re-expression exercise** Gets people out of their comfort/analytical zone to consider the feeling and emotions of the washing process.
2:00 pm		**Gym instructor and nutritionist** Discussion with fitness instructor and nutrition expert.	**Related worlds exercise** Creates new concepts based around fitness and nutrition. It also gives us lots of new vocabulary concepts.
3:30 pm		**Hairdresser** Half-hour talk on latest styles and tricks and tools of the trade from a top hairdresser.	**Related worlds exercise** The professional's view is very different from that of a major corporation.
4:30 pm		**What if game** Series of provocative statements designed to challenge current world perspective, e.g. 'What if products were twice the price?' 'What if you didn't need water?' 'What if shampoo didn't exist?' 'What if all products were solid?'	**Revolution exercise** Deliberate acts of provocation to focus people way outside the conventional market wisdom.

	ACTIVITY	PURPOSE
Day 2 8:30 am	**DIY** Participants washed their hair. One-third washed as normal, one-third with only one hand, one-third blindfolded.	**Re-expression exercise** Stops people talking and makes them 'do' instead. Direct experience provokes new ideas.
9:30 am	**Magazine beauty editor** The editor spends half an hour talking about the latest trends across the whole beauty market.	**Related worlds exercise** A completely fresh perspective from beyond the world of hair care but from categories with real relevance.
11:00 am	**Foreign hair care commercials** Ad agency shows a 20-minute video of hair care advertisements from countries outside Europe.	**Re-expression/related worlds exercise** Moves us from verbal to highly visual interpretation of our challenge with very different cultural interpretations.
12:00 noon	**Pottery class** A potter shows us about the moulding and shaping of clay. He includes tools and techniques for styling and colouring effects.	**Related worlds exercise** Fantastically rich related world for styling products. Just like people styling their hair, the potter needs 'body and hold'.

Day 2

Day 2

	ACTIVITY	PURPOSE
1:00 pm	**Random box** Whole series of random objects taken out of a box. Participants asked to make connections.	**Random links exercise** Freshness exercise designed to get us making connections and thinking outside the box of hair care.
2:00 pm	**Filtering and harvesting** Final two-hour session to give all the participants time to review the ideas generated.	Switching brain states from creative to more developmental/analytical.
4:00 pm	**Select leading ideas** Highlight areas for future development, pull out key learnings.	Gives everyone the chance to have their say.
5:00 pm	**Action/next steps** Focus on the key actions and next steps.	Maintains momentum and turns ideas into concrete business actions. Applications of project planning disciplines.

A two-day creative session like this takes a lot of energy to organise and needs a skilled facilitator. Imagine that you organised a similar session. Would you generate new ideas that your competitors hadn't even dreamed of?

Long-term freshness

So far we have concentrated on the day-to-day tools of creative thinking, the techniques that you can use straight away to radically improve the quality of your creative output. We know, however, from our own experience that this is only part of the picture. The skill of river-jumping allows you to make creative connections in a particular moment, but a lifetime of continual freshness will give your brain a store-cupboard of stimulus, allowing you to make free-flowing connections at any time.

The freshness store-cupboard is your store of internal mind stimulus. It comes from your unique experiences of life, and it will always stick with you to use in making connections whenever a creative challenge emerges. For us there are three types of idea, as shown in the model below. Ideas B and C can only come from planned stimulus, but idea type A can come at any time. And it is the quality of your own store-cupboard that dictates how good your free-flowing type A ideas will be.

Top of mind ideas. Sourced from your freshness store-cupboard	**A**	Automatic and intuitive
Ideas stimulated by river-jumping techniques	**B**	Brainstormed and planned
Ideas built upon by team members	**C**	Co-operative and interactive

There is no hierarchy at play here. A good idea is a good idea no matter where it comes from (although you will often have to use all three levels to get a real breakthrough business idea). The behaviour of the freshness store-cupboard gives you the ability to operate quickly, intuitively and spontaneously.

Let us explain

Most people follow set routines at work and even at home. The concept of the freshness store-cupboard recognises this fact and deliberately does something about it. It involves going out of your way (and out of your comfort zone) to experience new things, meet people you wouldn't normally come into contact with and to see the world from different perspectives. It involves making a deliberate break with your usual pattern of life.

Topping up the freshness store cupboard

Here are ten pattern-breaking ideas.

1. Take a new form of transport to work next week. You'll be amazed at who you'll meet and what you'll see.

2. Deliberately read a magazine or newspaper, listen to a radio station or watch a TV programme that you wouldn't normally (children's TV is good for this).

3. Plan a monthly lunch with people from other parts of the business you don't usually consult. Chat to them about an issue they are working on and get their perspectives on issues you are working on.

4. Get out of your normal environment for at least half a day a week. At least 70% of what we think is the result of what's around us.

5. Ask your family (especially kids) to help solve a problem you're working on.

6. Allocate twice as much time as you normally would to solving a problem. Make sure you have at least three solutions before you choose one.

7. Block out 'freshness time' for you and your team once a month. Go somewhere you wouldn't normally go together or do an activity you wouldn't normally do.

8. Take a walk in the park during office hours. Change the pace of your thinking. Take time to ponder.

9. Listen to the music charts. (Do you know what's number one at the moment?)

10. Reinvent your job role at least once a year.

This represents the start of creating a freshness habit. Rather than relying on willpower, create your own processes to make sure freshness is part of your life.

Breaking patterns is important because it provides a constant top-up of freshness. The freshness store-cupboard is kept well stocked by background stimulus. This means that when you need to be creative, you have a ready supply of freshness to draw on to make new connections. This is the first place you access when trying to have new ideas in the absence of stimulus. So how do you do it?

The tough part of pattern-breaking is that it forces you to move outside your comfort zone. The reason most of us got into patterns or rivers in the first place was because they make it easier to cope with the demands placed on us. At work, this is about the demands of our jobs, but for many of us this spills over into our home lives. At the weekend, you find you are more comfortable doing what you know than trying new things. Avoiding new situations becomes a coping strategy not just for work but for life. As we get older, and the demands on us multiply, most of us find we become more and more set in our ways. These patterns allow you to streamline your life – avoiding situations and people you don't regard as essential to the tasks you have to complete.

"An idea is a feat of association."

ROBERT FROST (1874–1963),
AMERICAN POET

Pattern-breaking turns this upside-down. It means making yourself do things you wouldn't normally do, or don't like doing. Faced with an invitation to meet new people or an opportunity to try something different, the logic of the accomplished pattern-breaker is: 'I'm not sure I'm going to enjoy this. Good, I'll do it anyway.' In this way, the pattern-breaker ensures a diet of fresh experiences. At a simple level, going to new places provides more freshness. Reading a different newspaper or listening to a different radio station puts stimulus in the cupboard for a rainy day.

It sounds easy. But we've discovered the hard way that pattern-breaking behaviour involves some serious discomfort. It means reprioritising – and that inevitably involves some pain. But pain with a purpose.

Freshness at ICI

ICI paints division has the look and feel of traditional big business. We were invited in to start breaking a few patterns. Ian Kenyon had just been appointed head of innovation. He had a clearly defined vision and a realisation that if ICI stayed firmly fixed in the world of paint it would never hit the stretching business targets set by the wider company. But all around him and his team surged the fast-flowing river of paint. Paint products; paint business targets; paint market research. They needed some fresh stimulus.

As part of our creative journey together, Ian, his team and ?What *If!* explored far beyond the world of paint. We set out to find some truly different related worlds. For example, we met a Colour Me Beautiful consultant who talked to us about how she matched colour to someone's skin tone and personality, then a colour psychologist who had a complex model matching personality types to tonal colour groups. (Interesting. Could we sell colour on personality types rather than simply names? London Retro Cool Colours range, for example, or English Country Lady range?)

A West End theatre lighting designer told us he could create any illusion with the use of light. (Interesting. Could we produce a range of paints that responded differently to different lighting conditions?) We met a fashion predictor – one of the people responsible for telling us that 'grey is the new black'! – while an interior decorator evangelised about how colour can change the mood. 'If I could paint the world,' he said, 'I could change how everyone feels!' Still more. An estate agent gave us tips for making a home more saleable. It's all about colour, smell, look, airflow (don't be fooled, this is a real art form!). We talked to an Australian computer programmer who had created the world's first commercial 'room on a screen' interface, allowing DIY enthusiasts to experiment on-screen rather than on their own walls.

The result of this work was a huge insight about how ICI wasn't really selling paint, but was in the mood creation business. This in itself opened up a number of exciting possibilities. One specific innovation was the creation of the world's first integrated home decorating solution. This system allows even the least accomplished decorator to integrate colours safely by sticking to a family of matching interiors which link colour on the walls to the décor around the room. Consumers can create a whole range of room feels with different fabric, paints and furniture on screen before making a final choice.

A success story in the making? We hope so. But don't underestimate these two important points: it takes awareness to realise you're stuck in a river in the first place – this is the first key step that Ian and his team took. Second, a journey into the unknown comes at a price. More time out of the office; the uncertainty of success; the questioning of others from a traditional business world who just don't get it. Stocking the freshness store-cupboard is a real investment. And, yes, it is worth it.

Structure in some freshness

At the individual level, you can bring some freshness into your working life by becoming a pattern-breaker. We've come across a number of enlightened companies that have put structures in place to support this kind of behaviour (there are some examples below). Most companies don't. Does yours?

Superquinn

Fergal Quinn, the charismatic founder of the Superquinn supermarket chain in Ireland, wants his people to stay fresh and creative about food and ways of selling it. So he set up a system whereby everyone in the company (right down to the shelf stackers) is responsible for reading one food-related magazine a month. Each employee is allocated a specific publication from around the world to read. Their job is to use it as stimulus and send Fergal any ideas or observations.

?What *If!*

Every two to three months we stop work for an afternoon. Responsibility for planning and organising our stimulus session is rotated so that everyone has a go. The guidelines are simple – the experience must involve the team doing something which we would never normally do and ideally stretch us. In these sessions we've: played bingo with pensioners in Kilburn, North London; drummed with African dancers; had our fortunes told; got tattooed (removable after two weeks); been on the world's scariest theme park rides; visited Japanese supermarkets; taken part in Shamanic rituals; had Reiki sessions; run a children's Christmas party… and so on. Nobody tries to explain what we will get out of it directly – it's understood, it's our freshness store-cupboard.

Ben & Jerry's

Ben & Jerry's Home-made Ice Cream is famous for its groovy flavours. Successes include Cherry Garcia, Chubby Hubby and Chunky Monkey. But coming up with new ideas year after year isn't easy. To stay fresh, the company has instituted 'Dessert Tours'. Folks from the R&D Kitchen go on annual culinary tours of leading American restaurants on the East and West Coasts, chatting to top chefs and customers to get insights from the leading edge of food. They ask what flavours and ingredients are popular this season, and could be big in the ice cream world next. The only guideline is that they must eat as many desserts as they physically can.

Southwest Airlines

A few years ago, Dallas-based Southwest introduced a scheme for people to spend one week every six months getting away from the office to have ideas about how the team was working and what they were focusing on. The scheme was so successful the practise is now encouraged across the whole of the business. Teams can go anywhere and do anything they like (within reason!) as long as they get stimulated to have ideas about how they can work most productively over the next six months.

Unilever

At Unilever Best Foods, a sophisticated freshness system has been designed. The 'germination process' as they call it, involves several people from every category team being nominated as stimulus hunters. Part of their role is to spend time out in the world searching for stimulus to jolt the rest of the team's thinking. Whole cupboards of stimulus are collected and used throughout a project. The germination process is formal, structured, with clear responsibility lines and agreed budgets. It is a clear demonstration of the company's commitment to the principle of freshness. In India, Unilever has a programme called 'Feel the Pulse', in which all of its 1500 managers go out of their offices, factories or labs for three days twice a year to 'look, listen and learn about consumers', by visiting their homes. All managers, not just sales and marketing managers, are included. It's a powerful way to enhance not only the consumer orientation of the company but to align managers across all functions.

Richer Sounds

Julian Richer, founder of UK hi-fi retailer Richer Sounds, has realised the benefits of getting employees out of the office. Each branch or department is expected to meet once a month. 'We don't pay for their time,' says Richer, 'but we give them £5 a head allowance for liquid refreshment.' His simple observation is that the primary thing employees have in common is their work. When they go out for a drink they eventually end up talking about their jobs. In the very different environment of the pub all sorts of fresh and innovative ideas start to emerge. Richer collects these using a simple ideas suggestion scheme.

Freshness – a final word

Our own experience at ?What *If!* is that structured 'freshness' experiences are no substitute for a stimulating life outside of work. We ask our people, 'How do you want to work? How can we fit around you?' The result is that many of our people negotiate their own contracts – preferring to take school holiday time off or have three or four day weekends. This flexibility comes at a cost to the employee (less salary) and means the resourcing of our project work is not always easy. However, the long-term payback of fresh employees buzzing with ideas, and very few leavers, easily outweighs any negatives. Admittedly this is easier to do for small companies but even if you work in a supertanker company just stop for a moment and ask yourself what if employee freshness was paramount? What could we do differently?

Summary

The brain is not set up to make creativity easy. That's because the brain is hard-wired to use an automatic and subconscious classification system based on past experiences. When it takes in a new piece of information it simply classifies and interprets it according to what it has experienced or seen like it before.

This system is highly effective and allows human beings to process huge amounts of information very quickly. But it also keeps us locked into current and past realities.

To break out of this limiting mode of thinking, we have to distract the brain from its current rules using stimulus. By focusing on a piece of stimulus, we can then find a connection back to the original problem which allows us to see it in a fresh way.

There are four river-jumping techniques.

Re-expression – finding an alternative way of describing or experiencing the issue.

Related worlds – finding an alternative but similar issue or benefit in another field.

Revolution – identifying then deliberately challenging the rules and assumptions.

Random links – using a deliberate connection with a random item.

In the longer term, deeper freshness can be achieved by building up a personal, 'freshness store-cupboard'. This begins when we deliberately break out of the patterns in our lives and fill our minds with varied and unusual experiences.

Finally, remember freshness and stimulus won't give you the idea itself, they are simply the raw material for a new connection.

greenhousing

Plants are at their most fragile when they are small and just starting to grow. That's why gardeners use greenhouses. It's the same with ideas. They are easiest to destroy when they first appear. Unfortunately, most business cultures tend to stifle ideas before they can take root.

Is this you?

◆ You offer an idea, but you are more often told why it won't work, rather than why it will.

◆ You notice that not all ideas in the business are given a real chance to grow.

◆ You are often so busy that you don't have time to discuss other people's bright ideas.

◆ You hear yourself or others using phrases like 'Yes, but …', 'We've tried that before …', or 'That won't work because…'

◆ There are some people in your business you really don't enjoy sharing your ideas with.

What is greenhousing?

A wise man was walking down a country lane when he happened upon a small genie sitting by the roadside. The genie smiled mischievously and confessed that as he had been discovered he must grant the man a wish. 'But to earn your wish', he said, 'you must first look at these two small shoots growing out of the ground and tell me which is the flower and which is the weed.'

The wise man asked the genie if there were any rules to the challenge. 'Only that the answer is your own, with the help of no one,' replied the genie. The next day the wise man arrived with some compost and a watering can and tended to the seedlings. Each day he returned and repeated his nurturing, until after a week he declared with total confidence, 'Genie, this is the flower, and this the weed.' The genie granted him his wish.

And so it is with ideas. Just as it's not obvious if seedlings will grow into weeds or flowers, so young ideas need time to grow and take root before you can judge their true worth.

Greenhousing is the behaviour that protects young ideas when they are at their most vulnerable, and nurtures them into healthy growth. It is an interactive behaviour that enables people to get the most out of their initial thinking by supporting each other's ideas.

Why do you need it? Because creativity needs a different environment from that driven by normal business behaviour.

Normal business behaviour is characterised by rapid-fire decisions – the ability to analyse swiftly and make sound judgements based on the available evidence. Analysis often involves an element of criticism and it's hard for young ideas to survive in this environment. If criticised or judged too soon, they wither and die. Have you ever offered a friend or colleague a new idea only to be greeted with the familiar response: 'Yes, but that wouldn't work because...' By engaging their critical reasoning skills they have already begun to squash the idea. There is no room left for it to grow.

Greenhousing is different. The critical faculties are suspended for a period and the seedling idea is given a chance to grow. All parties simply engage in nurturing ideas, spending time making them as good as possible. Greenhousing is fun, supportive and energising, but it also requires real discipline. You have to hold back those analytical thoughts and positively explore the new ideas. Eventually these ideas can be exposed to sound business judgement, but not until they have grown a little first. Ideas do not emerge fully formed.

"A new idea is delicate. It can be killed by a sneer or a yawn; it can be stabbed to death by a joke, or worried to death by a frown on the right person's brow."

CHARLES BROWER

The reason greenhousing is so important is that creativity is rarely a sudden flash of inspiration leading to the perfect invention. Greenhousing is the nurturing behaviour that helps teams grow strong ideas. We believe that greenhousing behaviour is at the heart of creativity in business.

Why greenhousing matters

In recent years our working lives have become a daily round of priority-setting: 'to do' lists; calls made; decisions taken; boxes ticked. We have become incredible task-performing human beings – or 'human-doings', as the latest buzzword puts it.

So frenetic has it become that today's business world often feels like an **Emergency Room (ER)** at a hospital – rapid-fire analysis of the situation, judgement, precise decision, prompt action. This is the way we work most of the time. And it's absolutely vital for the success of business and for the implementation of competitive innovation – but not on its own.

The problem is that the ER thinking style has become so automatic it dominates most company cultures. Often, it is the only approach that is recognised and rewarded. But the ER environment on its own is hugely damaging to the growth of new ideas. If it is applied too early, it acts like poison on seedling ideas.

Try monitoring yourself over the next few days to observe what your first instinct is when you hear a new idea. For most business people, it will be a knee-jerk reaction to judge. The first question that pops into most of our heads is, 'Is this a good or bad idea?' closely followed by, 'What's wrong with it? Are there any holes in the logic? Is it practical?'

A classic symptom of this is the tendency to apply the ER interrogation to our own fragile ideas before they have been fully expressed. How many times have you heard yourself, or others, start to describe an idea and then, even before the sentence is finished, explain the reasons why it wouldn't work?

But ER judgement isn't just a by-product of high pressure business culture. The reason it's so difficult to switch out of is that it's a cultural norm that's existed for thousands of years.

Back to our ER roots

Philosophers back in Ancient Greece, lacking the skills and tools to test the world around them scientifically, were left simply to theorise and guess about the nature of existence. Eventually a theory would be proposed and it was then the duty of all others to critique and challenge the version of reality which had been presented. If, after serious challenge, the theory still seemed to hold, it would be accepted as a 'truth' until someone could offer a better theory.

This logical, combative thinking approach, relying as it does on the development of sharpened critical facilities, became the dominant style employed in our education system. From the moment we go to school, we are trained in the discipline of finding a right or wrong answer.

But in the initial stage of creativity, there is no right or wrong answer, there are only, and always, alternatives! Sadly, we have been trained – and are training the next generation – never to look for them.

The modern ER culture

The ER culture is all around us. Turn on your radio and tune into a news or current affairs programme. In most cases the aim of the interviewer is to find out what's wrong with what the other person says. The line of questioning is designed to cause the maximum friction, and prove the interviewee wrong. The theory is that this confrontational questioning style uncovers the facts so that members of the audience can make up their own minds. But the proponents of this approach rarely take the time to explore the real meaning, value or goodwill behind the intention. Ideas are not fully explored.

The political world can provide dramatic examples of the negative aspects of ER culture. So much of what we know of politics is little more than judgemental mud slinging – picking holes in arguments and criticising the people behind the arguments. Elections are won on 'negative campaigning' alone, often with little or nothing by way of positive ideas.

There has to be a better way. Imagine a politician being interviewed in the greenhouse style, talking with other experts, building ideas and making life better. Imagine hearing the politician say, 'Hey, I'd never thought of it like that before, what a great idea we've developed.' The level of creative debate could soar. To do this, however, they would have to let go of the ER instinct that demands immediate judgement.

Because of ER instincts, most things in the public domain have minimal creative content. As a society, we force our most brilliant people to create behind closed doors, and then we complain about secrecy when they do. If there are media people reading this book now, here's an idea that could give you a unique selling position. Call your column or programme 'The Greenhouse' and dedicate it to the growth of ideas. Set up a non-judgemental, supportive atmosphere. Invite celebrities to discuss their new ideas. Someone has to make a start.

The 10 best phrases to kill an idea
1. *"Yes, but..."*
2. *"We've tried it before..."*
3. *"That won't work because..."*
4. *"Have you really thought about the implications..."*
5. *"We don't have time for this right now..."*
6. *"Put it down on paper..."*
7. *"Exactly how much is this idea of yours worth?"*

8. *"Please do a cost benefit analysis and then we'll talk abut it..."*
9. *"OK, I hear you but we've just invested millions in doing it another way..."*
10. *"That's fine in theory, but it doesn't work like that..."*

Why the ER and the greenhouse don't mix

Greenhousing plays a vital role in the development of creative ideas and cultures; however, injecting it into your business is not easy. Most people start by trying to be more greenhouse-like in their day-to-day ER interaction. Unfortunately this can create more problems.

A real greenhouse is a total environment. Gardeners don't open the greenhouse door on a cold night to see what might happen. The world of ER and greenhousing are different worlds, and they mix like oil and water. They are characterised by different ways of thinking and behaving that completely cut across each other. Getting the benefits of greenhousing requires adding a completely new and separate set of skills and behaviours to your existing ER ones. Both are vital, but you can only use one at a time.

Greenhousing is not understood very well in modern business. Many business people have never experienced a truly non-analytical, energised, 'building' experience at work. Starved of this experience, they react to ideas the only way they know how – by judging them. This can lead to extreme frustration. The person judging the idea is often just trying to help but the person having the idea (often unconsciously) begins to feel defensive. The result is a downward spiral.

Think of your own experience. In a meeting, you offer an idea that is immediately analysed by other people. The majority of the group may be in greenhouse mode, but it takes only one person to stay in analytical mode and the creative buzz is lost. The short-term effect of mixing these two worlds together is that ideas do not get properly developed.

In the longer term, the effects are even more pernicious. People, bruised by the constant knocking of their ideas, stop offering the first thoughts that are so crucial to success in competitive business environments. It is the long-term effect that is the most damaging. For some people it can take a lot of reassurance to get them to offer their creative ideas again to the organisation.

Great efforts are being made in the business community to build creative confidence. That confidence has been analysed and judged out of the workforce by a business culture that does not understand the management skills involved in directing the human imagination.

Watching a film with a cynic – negative buzz

Ever watched a movie with a cynic? Someone who seems totally unable to suspend disbelief for long enough to enjoy what is intended to be an entertaining piece of make-believe. You have to put up with a constant stream of comments about how unbelievable the story is; how far-fetched the characters are; how completely implausible it is that they should behave that way. Irritating, isn't it? That's what it feels like to share ideas with someone who is stuck in the ER environment. It's bad enough when it's a film or a book. But when the ideas are yours, you are bound to take their negative comments personally. It doesn't have to be this way. But to change it requires organisations and the people who work for them to master new skills and techniques. In short, to practise greenhousing behaviour.

The rest of this chapter will focus on living in the greenhouse. Remember, when you're in there you must stick to the rules with no exceptions. There is no middle ground.

But before you rush headlong into your new world it's advisable to check if that's where you want to be. For our 'greenhouse test' we use two quick checks.

First, what sort of behaviour is required? Do we need a decision, to share information, to judge a proposal or develop an idea? If it is the latter, go to the greenhouse. Otherwise, stay in the ER.

Second, where is the person I am talking to? If he or she is in the greenhouse, you will need to apply the behaviours in this section. If the person is still in the ER and you want them to come with you to the greenhouse, you must signal your intent so that they know the rules you're playing by.

Some of history's worst ER blind spots

'I think there is a world market for maybe five computers.'
Thomas Watson JR, Head of IBM 1956–1970

'Who the hell wants to hear actors talk?'
Harry M Warner, Warner Brothers, 1927

'We don't like their sound. Groups of guitars are on their way out.'
Decca Records rejecting The Beatles, 1962

'Television won't be able to hold on to any market it captures in the first six months. People will soon get tired of staring at a plywood box every night.'
Daryl F Zanuck, Head of 20th Century Fox, 1946

'Everything that can be invented has been invented.'
Charles H Duell, Commissioner of Patents, 1899

Being in the SUN

The model we use to get people started greenhousing is a simple one. In the natural world, the sun is the energy that drives all living things. Through photosynthesis in plants, it creates the basic fuel for life. The whole point of a greenhouse is that it lets in the sun's energy and keeps out the rain and other harsh weather conditions that could damage the plants while they are at their most delicate. You can think of greenhousing behaviour as creating an environment that lets in the sun and keeps out the rain.

SUN = Suspend + Understand + Nurture
RAIN = React + Assume + INsist

For the majority of us, it's all too easy to let the **RAIN** into a creative situation. When we first hear an idea, our instinct is to **react** quickly, to let our analytical skills cut loose. We rarely take the time to check that we really understand what the other person means. We **assume** that we know, and immediately start to judge it. Once it's started raining, other people tend to join in. Listening to your judgement of their idea, the idea giver gets defensive and starts to **insist** that the idea is right. You play your part by insisting back. The insisting passes backwards and forwards over the net like a tennis match, with the emotional strokes often getting harder, as each tries to smash the other person's argument and win the point.

In **SUN** mode we **suspend** judgement. Neither participant is trying to score points. The tennis match becomes a deliberate attempt to keep the ball in play, to **understand** and **nurture**. What follows is an enjoyable and invigorating rally, where both players exercise their skill and wits in keeping the ball moving.

Let's look at this model in detail.

Three stages of staying in the SUN

1 · Suspending judgement

The first step of greenhousing is to suspend judgement. This requires the ability to consciously step away from forming an instant opinion. It's very difficult to do. You have to consciously disengage your mind from the normal ER response.

So when you hear an idea, stop. Pause... Now consciously choose to remove yourself from the ER environment. Don't worry whether it's a good or bad idea. It doesn't matter at this stage. The important thing is to suspend prejudice.

Let go of your critical faculty. Simply allow the thought to exist without evaluating it. Think of it as putting judgement in neutral for a while. Remember, you are not signing up to do anything except explore the idea.

The reason you have to do this in a very conscious way is because you've been trained to judge. But suspended judgement actually takes the pressure off you. You don't have to have an answer!

You're probably judging what you're reading right now. Don't. Just go with it. Open your mind and explore the ideas here. Leave the door open to the possibility and live with it for a while.

You might well be asking, 'If I'm not judging, what am I doing instead?' This is where the other two elements of greenhousing come in – understanding and nurturing.

No zingers allowed

Some companies have developed their own structures to support the suspension of judgement. For example, in the US, Southwest Airlines' 'University of People' is an official 'no zinger' zone. Zingers, in Southwest parlance, are 'undermining, critical or judgemental comments'. In group discussions, because there is a high level of consciousness around positive nurturing behaviour, if zingers happen they are quickly and easily dealt with.

2 · Understanding

The second behaviour of greenhousing comes after you've suspended judgement – now you have to understand, and see the world through the other person's eyes.

Ask yourself whether you really know what they're talking about. You may have got the gist of it, but make a real effort to understand the idea – and the point of view that gave rise to it. Try to stand in the other person's shoes and understand how they see the idea, why they are motivated by it, what makes it good for them and why.

Understanding often simply involves empathy, using open questions to explore what lies behind the thought (what you've heard is probably the outcome of their thinking process). If you can tune into their mental wavelength, and really understand why they have said what they've said, then you are in a much better position to support it.

Try these.

1. *"Tell me more."*
2. *"Why are you so excited about the idea?"*
3. *"How's it different to the way the world is now?"*
4. *"How did you get the idea/where did it come from?"*
5. *"What would it look like?"*
6. *"What do I stop doing in order to do what you're suggesting?"*
7. *"How would I tell someone else the good things about this idea?"*
8. *"What would the positive consequences be?"*

The greatest skill involved here is that of listening to the answer. It's hard work. Keep checking what you think they have said to be sure you really understand it.

3 · Nurturing

The effect of practising the first two behaviours of the SUN model is to create a supportive environment for people to share their ideas. However, this is not enough to produce ideas strong enough to leave the greenhouse. The final stage, **nurturing**, is about building stronger ideas.

In business, ideas rarely come from a single flash of inspiration – they need to be built and developed. Without this, creativity can feel like fun, but is ultimately a wasteful indulgence; because the ideas lack development, their potential is never revealed.

You can see this happening in brainstorms where lots of ideas are produced but no one stops to build any of them into a big idea. The output is a huge list of disconnected thoughts that rarely get followed through. Competitive innovation is about building up ideas – so we need to go and grow green, nurturing fingers!

Practically we identify three key elements to **nurturing**.

(a) Make it better or 'build it' – Don't just understand ideas. Set out to grow them. For example, let's say you work for an ice cream company and you're out to dinner with some friends. One tells you that she thinks that an after-dinner ice cream would be a terrific new idea. Your first response (ER) is to think: 'Oh no, I'm not at work now; and this isn't a new idea anyway.' But you catch yourself, suspend your judgement and ask some questions like, 'That sounds interesting Laura, what made you think of that?'

The chocolates were being passed round at the time, and Laura confesses that she fancies something a little cooler. The idea came from a box of chocolates. Now build on the idea – the ice cream could come in a box like sweets – have different centres – you could use Belgian chocolate. Can you feel the idea building? (You don't have to make any decisions yet; you're just relaxing to see where it goes.)

(b) Seek value/find an angle – If you can't think of a building block that takes an idea to the next level, try to see if there's anything in the idea that you particularly like. Look for a principle, or concept; try to discover if there is any part of the idea that has value. Let's take our ice cream example again: you've got an idea about ice cream being packaged like sweets, with different centres and different types of chocolate. What is it about this idea that's interesting?

Well, sweets are portable and convenient, and kids like their variety. Maybe there's an idea here about mini ice creams packaged like sweets? Then you remember a small piece of market research last year where mums were complaining about ice cream getting everywhere – on the kids' faces, clothes, push chairs. This could be an idea worth progressing. This is SUN in action.

The transistor radio

Ever wonder why the Japanese are so brilliant at adapting technology? It's because they see the idea within the idea; they have insight. While it was the British who invented the transistor, it was the Japanese who recognised that the idea within the idea was small electronics for mainstream consumers. Based on this insight, the transistor radio was born – one of the founding blocks of Japan's micro-electronic revolution.

Often people only take ideas at face value. Your objective should be to become a detective, developing your insight, constantly looking for the idea within the idea.

(c) Find alternatives – Keep pushing yourself to find another way to do things. This behaviour works against the grain for many people in business, because the need to do **now** dominates the need to do **smart**. However, the habit of forcing yourself to spend time in exploring alternatives can very quickly change this.

Let's go back to our ice cream. We started off with chocolate box and mini ice cream sweets for kids, but what else is there? Look for the idea within the idea. Chocolate box ice creams could be re-expressed as ice cream gifts.

Where does this take you? What about ice cream rock with the name of your recipient inside – sculptured ice cream cake as an impressive after-dinner desert – an ice cream game you could play after dinner and eat? Each of these has the potential to be a new source of ideas ready for more greenhousing.

The nurturing behaviour that is greenhousing is an underrated creative force. It relies on building, seeking value and finding alternatives.

Snapshots

The following is a real example of greenhousing that led to the launch in 1999 of Snapshots – the world's first flavoured, carbonated spirit sold in a shot glass.

This is a recollection of two or three minutes of a stimulus and ideas session we ran with the senior marketing and development team at Bass Brewing in the UK, when the energy just seemed to flow. We blindfolded the team and gave them a series of weird and wonderful taste experiences – from cold baked beans to chilli peppers to chocolate.

The idea was to get them to think about alternatives to the traditional drinks experience. One specific stimulus was an ice cube made from pure lemon juice. The moment it exploded on the taste buds people spat it out, shocked and wondering what sadistic maniacs had convinced them to do this; but they suspended their judgement, which allowed them to explore what could be. The conversation went like this...

Conversation	Commentary
'Yeuch. I'd never drink that in a month of Sundays.'	Initial strong reaction
'OK, OK, but what principle could you steal from this to create a new drink?'	Suspend judgement and explore
'Well, it's certainly a shock to the system.'	State principle
'Yeah, it goes straight to the back of your head.'	Understand and explore
'I like that – a drink that goes straight to the back of your head. Feels like a big head rush.'	Nurture and build
'Like champagne with sugar and brandy; the bubbles go straight to your head.'	Explore
'So, what if you could put pure bubbles in someone's mouth?'	Nurture
'Then down them in one, like a tequila shot.'	Build
'You'd sell it in a shot glass. You know, like the girls in the Mexican bars.'	Understand and explore
'So what we've got is a champagne slammer sold in a shot glass.'	Build
'Yeah, only it could be vodka. It's much cooler.'	Build
'And you'd probably flavour it as well.'	Build

This is what you want more of, and what's really great is that by the end of the session it's no longer just one person's idea, it's the team's idea. This is 'ideas democracy' in action. The result of this two minutes of greenhousing was a flavoured vodka drink sold in a shot glass. It was launched nine months later.

SUNdays at work

Our mission at ?What If! is to help people in business understand that there are two worlds within business – the ER and the greenhouse. Each has a different behaviour and thinking style. By being aware you can consciously switch from one world to the other at the appropriate time.

At a personal level, greenhousing behaviour is playful and filled with the energy of growth; a safe place that offers protection from the sometimes harsh, judgemental climate outside. Yet it has a sense of excitement and energy we call the 'positive buzz' of creation. A sure sign of positive buzz is when you get to the end of a creative session and it's impossible, and irrelevant, to distinguish whose ideas were whose.

At a cultural organisational level, greenhousing behaviour builds creative capacity and confidence over a period of time. Like a Mexican wave flowing through a sports stadium, greenhousing is an inclusive behaviour, involving everyone.

 A greenhousing culture supports the release of an organisation's creative potential.

A ridiculous idea

In the early 1990s, a police task force was set up to tackle the rising tide of burglaries and theft in the UK. In a moment of inspired lateral thinking, the revolutionary thought was that criminals be persuaded to identify themselves. The idea was radical – crazy, even – but rather than crush it, the idea was built on. How could the police get criminals to turn themselves in? What would tempt them to incriminate themselves? Further discussions led to the brainwave of placing 'Wanted' advertisements in local newspapers, offering cash for a quantity of televisions, video players and other household items popular with burglars and petty criminals. The ads attracted truckloads of the stolen goods – driven by the very people the police wanted to catch up with. The sting was a great success, not just because someone had the wild idea that criminals could be persuaded to turn themselves in, but because the initial idea wasn't laughed out of existence – it was nurtured.

Sun and rain recap

☺   ☹

S

Suspend

The two-minute pause – every time you hear an idea you practise this drill.

Visualise yourself giving the idea rather than receiving it.

Give out positive energy.

React

React quickly with a view of your own.

Remain in opposition; your focus is on your own arguments.

Just do the above, and the negative energy will take care of itself.

R

U

Understand

Really try to get inside the other person's head with open questions: 'Tell me more...' 'Let me understand...' 'What else do you like about your idea...?' Great listening.

Paraphrase what you think they mean, and check you've got it right: 'So are you saying that...'

Assume

Keep thinking about your own agenda.

Assume you know: 'I think...' 'I know that...' 'I only meant...'

Listen in order to pick holes in their argument/idea.

A

N

Nurture

Make it better by 'building': 'So if you think X, maybe we could do X and Y.'

Seek value/find an angle 'What's the big idea behind this idea.'

Find alternatives: 'How else could we do this?'

Insist

Find fault or 'knock': 'That will never work.'

Find another flaw in the idea and insist you're right. 'I know that won't work, we've tried it before.'

Insist that there is only one way to do it.

IN

When to greenhouse?

The formal greenhouse

Most people will have experienced a greenhouse environment in a formal setting. A planned brainstorming session, for example, is a formal greenhouse with its own set of rules (be positive, build ideas, have fun, etc.). It's a big greenhouse with plenty of room for many people inside.

Other examples of this include fixed agenda items in meetings. The group sets aside a part of the agenda to generate ideas on a particular subject. Some companies have taken this principle a little further than most, with a specific number of days set aside every month for individual creative time.

Similarly, some businesses have specially designated physical environments that they devote entirely to greenhouse behaviour. In 1998 Heinz converted a cottage in its UK Head Office grounds into a creative play space, complete with the material and the behaviours appropriate to greenhousing.

These formal greenhouse spaces – whether they exist in a physical or virtual sense – provide a very clear framework in which people can let their hair down and be creative. But greenhousing doesn't have to be restricted to a formal setting. You can also put a temporary greenhouse over a conversation that lasts just a few minutes in an ordinary working day.

The pocket greenhouse

There is another sort of greenhousing that is much harder to practise. This involves informal sessions, often just between two people, that occur during the normal working day. The skill in informal greenhousing lies in recognising a creative situation and putting up a pocket greenhouse on the spot.

Accomplished 'greenhousers' can switch out of an ER environment and change their behaviour to go into a pocket greenhouse when required. Think of them as being skilled at placing a temporary 'nurture bubble' over a conversation. It's not easy because it means seeking value in what at first might appear to be a ridiculous idea. It requires a basic sense of respect for the other person and an understanding that you are greenhousing their creative potential, not necessarily the immediate idea. Such a pocket greenhouse or nurture bubble also needs great signalling – a behaviour we explore later.

The organisational greenhouse

When we talk to our clients about greenhousing they say something like this: 'Greenhousing sounds sensible. We understand that in order for our new products to be truly innovative we'll need to nurture our seedling ideas properly. At the moment this is not our behaviour – we tend to leap to judgement and action. But the issue for us is that it sounds expensive and fuzzy. How long do we have to greenhouse for? How do we know when to stop greenhousing and start moving ideas and concepts through our innovation decision process?'

It's a good question. All organisations have limited resources. None can afford to live in a protective nurturing world forever. Our response is two-fold. Firstly, some greenhousing is better than none and often a little will go along way. An hour spent really seeking value is rarely wasted. Plan in a small amount of greenhousing. See how it feels. Judge it by its results. Next time do more. Our second response is to help our clients develop simple structures that make greenhousing an inevitable behaviour prior to judging. Try these next time your finance director asks for the discounted cash flow yield on your latest idea.

◆ *"We need to spend three hours in the greenhouse before I can answer your questions about yield?"*
◆ *"Our innovation rule is to have at least one off-site session with consumers before we expose the idea to the company's judgement tools."*
◆ *"Before we move on in this project I want two alternatives."*

Another key structure to support a shift in behaviour is to change language. Rather than waiting for language to shift, make it change by creating an explicit phrasebook of the new language you want to hear. By driving the language into the culture you'll be amazed at how quickly the shift to greenhousing begins to take effect. Try these next time you're presented with a seedling idea.

◆ *"There's something really interesting in what you're saying."*
◆ *"Let's go for it anyway…"*
◆ *"How can we make this better…?"*
◆ *"My build on your idea is…"*
◆ *"Let's push this further…"*
◆ *"What I like in the idea is…"*
◆ *"The principle here that I like is…"*

This simple response recognises that although you don't fully understand someone's idea there's maybe some gold in it. It gives permission to carry on and explore without committing anyone to accept the idea. Creating your own language like this will facilitate the suspension of judgement. These are circuit breakers designed to tune us in to the new idea. They force people to make ideas better and prevent them from slipping into judgement. Too often people see only the idea in front of them. These phrases ensure people look deeper for value in an idea.

Red card/yellow card

At the brewing company Bass, a traditionally robust male culture where sarcasm is a cultural norm, nurturing behaviour is supported by language borrowed from sport. When we explained greenhousing we were told that the traditional Bass culture was resistant to what the company's managers called 'London Agency-Speak'. Instead, they adopted a football analogy for individuals who trample on ideas. During a football match, players who commit a foul are shown different colour cards by the referee to indicate the seriousness of the offence. Bass adopted a similar language. A simple warning is a yellow card (equivalent to a booking). A second offence or a particularly negative comment gets a red card (equivalent to being sent off) and the offender has to leave the meeting. It's done very playfully, but there is a really serious intent behind it.

A lifelong challenge

Armed with the principles of greenhousing and with the presence of a little goodwill, we have seen individuals and organisations significantly increase the creative buzz in their working lives. We believe that anyone with an open mind, who works in a supportive environment where the principles of greenhousing are understood, will be able to work successfully in SUN.

Once you become aware of your in-built behaviour of judging or analysing, it is not too difficult to catch yourself, stop doing it, and allow a creative exchange to grow. However, for those who really want to develop their creative skills and get all they possibly can from this book, it is always possible to push greenhousing even further.

So far we have talked about greenhousing in relatively easy conditions. Someone offers an idea and you respond in SUN. They pick up on this and come back with more SUN behaviours. This type of interaction is much easier in a 'formal greenhouse' (like a brainstorm session), where the environment is predictable. However pocket greenhousing requires a far greater degree of skill because in business, as with weather, the climate is constantly changing. In business, as in life, it could RAIN at any time.

Metaphorically, it RAINs in our heads many times a day, and when it happens we find it much harder to practise greenhouse behaviours. So our challenge to create involves seeking to reduce day-by-day, year-by-year, the occasions when it RAINs, because this is what will stop us expanding creative potential. We call this expanding our 'ideas bandwidth'.

Everyone has their own idea of what the world is like, shaped by opinions, values, prejudice and assumptions. Think of this as a bandwidth in the mind. When we hear an idea that fits inside our existing bandwidth, we find it much easier to respond to openly. In such circumstances, it is much easier to operate with SUN behaviours and to create.

It's when we hear an idea or opinion, see a behaviour, or meet a person who doesn't match our expectation that the real challenge occurs. When this happens, often we react by becoming defensive. From this position it's incredibly hard to create anything new, because the focus of our energy is directed at defending our existing position. It starts to RAIN.

The challenge for those who wish to truly excel in the practise of creative behaviour is to react in this way less and less. This requires us to learn how to turn the RAIN off in our heads when we feel the first few drops begin to fall. To do this it's essential to recognise the signs of RAIN. If you feel any of the sensations below, it's often an early warning signal that RAIN is coming:

1. *Losing your temper.*
2. *Feeling frustrated.*
3. *Insecurity about the situation.*
4. *Insecurity about yourself.*
5. *Lack of respect for the person you're dealing with.*
6. *Strong sense you're right (because you're an expert).*
7. *Overreacting to criticism.*
8. *Leaping to judgement.*
9. *Justifying your idea.*
10. *Rushing to tell the person they're wrong.*

So what do you do in these circumstances? First pause (count to three), give yourself a few seconds to take stock and switch from RAIN to SUN. The act of pausing then switching is critical to avoiding automatic RAIN behaviour.

But remember, moving into SUN mode doesn't necessarily mean you agree with someone else's idea. You can spend time in the SUN and then switch back into the ER world to assess after you've created. What it does mean is that you're always willing to make a choice to explore.

It probably won't come as a surprise to you that those people who find it hardest to remain in the SUN state – to remain open to creative possibility – are those who have a very narrow or fixed view of the world, which they hold onto at all costs. Because they have a narrow personal bandwidth, it is frequently being challenged as life happens around them.

It is even more difficult to remain in SUN state when you do not fully respect the people working around you. Lack of respect for others is one of the most fundamental barriers to SUN behaviour and creative potential.

From our own work in this area, we are well aware of just how difficult it is to stay open and in the SUN. But the benefits are enormous for those who have the personal bravery and strength of character not to get drawn into their own instinctive RAIN patterns. SUN behaviour allows you to open up your own and others' full creative potential – to engage with those around you and take the full value from those interactions. Over time, it enables you and others to expand your collective ideas bandwidth beyond its existing limits.

If you are inspired by this challenge, start taking notice of when the RAIN begins in you. Stop and make a choice to spend some time in the SUN/greenhouse.

The skill is to recognise that an idea is simply a stepping-off point. It provides a seed for creative growth. The more an idea challenges your thinking, the greater the potential to grow it into something that has never been seen before. Understanding this and not feeling threatened by ideas boosts personal creativity. SUN behaviour nourishes all ideas.

> *"An idea is a point of departure and no more. As soon as you elaborate it, it becomes transformed by thought."*
>
> PABLO PICASSO (1881–1973)

Summary

Young ideas are easy to destroy, especially in the over dominant ER world of business.

There is another approach – the complementary skills set of nurturing and growing ideas – greenhousing.

Business cultures often do not reward, and frequently do not even recognise, the existence of this alternative way. As a result, ideas remain underdeveloped and people hold back their creativity – saving it for the weekends.

Our vision of the future is to encourage people in business to switch between the ER and the greenhouse at the appropriate creative moment. This means being in the SUN and staying out of the RAIN.

Suspend judgement
Understand
Nurture

React
Assume
INsist

Greenhousing is not halfway behaviour; you must be right in the greenhouse with the door closed.

The obvious greenhousing structure is a brainstorm. However, it can be applied to any conversation. Be ready to put up your pocket greenhouse. Use language to shift your culture into greenhousing; create an explicit phrasebook.

Work on your ideas bandwidth. Learn to catch those moments of automatic RAIN behaviours more often. Make a choice to explore and expand your bandwidth.

realness

Why don't people get excited about your ideas at work? Even when you think you're really onto something, they just don't seem passionate. No matter how well you think you explained your idea, they just don't 'get it'.

Is this you?

◆ **You talk a lot.**

◆ **Your meetings are filled with presentation slides, bullet points, spreadsheets, words, numbers and more words.**

◆ **You and your people are distant from the world in which your consumers make decisions.**

◆ **Your interests and skills outside of work are rarely used in your professional life.**

◆ **You rarely go home at night and show your family or friends what you've been working on and say, 'Hey, look what I did today!'**

Get real

Realness is a simple but powerful concept. It demands that we ask of our idea: 'How can we make it real right now?'

Realness is about getting as close to a real customer experience as you can. It's a state of mind throughout the whole creative process. It says that no matter how partially formed your idea is you are always striving to reproduce whatever you offer in the way in which your customer really experiences it. It doesn't matter whether you are selling a product or a service, or if your market is a few people or a million people, realness will always give you new insights and make ideas better.

It's fun, fast and for most of us it involves a real revolution in the way we work. But rather than talk about realness – let's get real with some examples!

Credit card realness

Recently, we were presenting an idea for a radically new sort of credit card to a group of managers from a financial services company, which included the divisional director. Our basic idea was that all sorts of benefits and information could be offered on one single card. It would do more than just offer credit. Health insurance, vehicle recovery and a variety of other services would also be included. Our client was sceptical. Could these disparate benefits fit together under one single card and concept? We attempted to explain why we believed consumers would readily accept the idea, but the client just wasn't convinced.

So we produced a prototype; a fully mocked-up version of the new credit card, complete with magnetic strip and an embossed account number. When our client saw it, the whole tone of the meeting changed. Suddenly, the director became animated, passionate even. He was holding the answer in his hand. He 'got it', and his colleagues got it too. For the rest of the meeting, he kept picking up the prototype, touching it, and looking at it. For him, the idea had become real and he was going to make it happen.

Tiger realness

In 1998, Disney opened its new $1 billion theme park, Animal Kingdom, in Orlando, Florida. Five times bigger than the original Disneyland in California, Animal Kingdom represents the most important addition to the Florida Disneyworld location since the opening of the Disney/MGM Studios in 1989. But the new theme park nearly didn't get built at all. CEO Michael Eisner liked the idea, but the strategic planners around him weren't convinced. They could only imagine a variation on the traditional zoo. To make matters worse, it coincided with the recession of the early 1990s and the theme park business was suffering.

The champions of the new park, the famous Walt Disney Imagineers, were undeterred. This eclectic bunch of designers, artists, writers and engineers has been recreating the Disney magic ever since Walt himself sketched out the original plan for Disneyland. Heading up the design team was Imagineer Joe Rohde. It was his job to convince the planners that Animal Kingdom would be a radical improvement on the traditional zoo. He spent months trying to win approval for the new theme park. But meeting after meeting failed to persuade the doubters. Finally, when Eisner wondered out loud whether the mere sight of live animals would be sufficient to excite visitors, Rohde decided it was time to introduce some realness into what was fast becoming a theoretical debate.

At the next meeting, he brought with him a live 400-pound Bengal tiger. When presented with the power of the real experience, any intellectual debate about whether animals are or aren't exciting evaporated. Animal Kingdom got the green light.

(Gunther, Marc, & McGowan, Joe, 'Disney's Call of the Wild', *Fortune*, 13 April 1998)

What holds realness back?

Realness is the art of bringing an idea to life in whatever way you can rather than relying solely on words and memos. The Disney tiger and the credit card story are exceptional in business. We find that most organisations have little awareness of the benefits and practise of realness. Instead, they have unwittingly created cultures where the medium of communication is primarily the written or spoken word.

There is nothing wrong with words. Words are wonderful tools used in the right way at the right time. The accuracy and efficiency of communication needed in the ER environment suits bullet points, memos and e-mails. But when it comes to creativity, 'word-only cultures' act as a barrier to innovation. Once you've decided to go into the greenhouse and into the SUN, words alone just aren't enough.

We have a saying at ?What If!: 'If you are not selling words then don't invent with them!' Like us, you've probably been in too many meetings with too much theoretical debate producing hot air about a new product or service.

Consumers (customers, clients, however you define them) will never experience this debate. They will make up their minds about the real thing, the product of the debate. The point is that the medium really is the message. Disney's message was the wondrous power of animals like the tiger. Debate got nowhere until the medium changed to 'Tiger!' Similarly with the credit card story, we could have talked all day, trying to picture a consumer's reaction to the new cards. But it was only when we changed the medium and made it 'real', that the new card came alive.

Let's leave the world of business briefly and think about people we all consider to be highly creative – artists and inventors. Have you ever heard of an artist writing a report to explain his work? They leave that to the critics while they get on with creating. How about an inventor? They produce a prototype (a word we are going to use a lot more of in this section). It may be made from cardboard and held together with an elastic band, but it's a prototype all the same. They instinctively know that the act of making it real, rather than writing a memo, will make the idea better and help convince themselves and others it is possible.

The saying that a picture is worth a thousand words is very true for creative behaviour. The beauty of a song or a picture is that it conveys the real essence of the idea and impacts deeply on our imagination. It 'touches us'.

"What I hear I forget, what I see I remember, what I do I know."
CHINESE PROVERB

Literature aside, words are middlemen. Someone could describe a painting by Van Gogh to you but it would be a poor substitute for seeing the real thing yourself. The same applies to creative interchanges.

In this section we'll look at the exciting and enlightening world of realness.

Why words fail us

The Western education system is based primarily on words. From an early age we are encouraged to draw, sing and act at school, but these make up a tiny part of the curriculum compared to words. By the time we leave school our success is often judged solely on our ability to communicate using language.

Like many of the other behaviours mentioned in this book, this has enormous advantages for business. However, when it comes to creativity we have found that often words fail us. They do so for three reasons.

1 · Theatre of the mind

When we are communicating simple facts and figures, words are an efficient way of ensuring everyone understands the same basic information simply and quickly. However, when we start to try to describe creative concepts our words are open to interpretation. That's the beauty of radio or books. We all interpret the story differently. We all get it but we all get it differently. We have a theatre inside our heads – each of us seeing and feeling things differently. (Remember how the brain classifies according to past experience? Past experience affects what we see in our mind's eye.)

So, if I'm trying to get you to help build or even buy into my idea and all I'm doing is showing you a chart with a few bullet points, then I'm reducing the chances that you will 'get it'. I have no guarantee that the image forming in your head is the same as the one I'm trying to communicate. What makes this all the more tricky is that when I explain my idea, I don't know whether you're reacting to what I meant or to your own interpretation of it. Using words as a creative medium can cause ideas to fall at the first hurdle – people either don't get it or they get the wrong thing. Catch yourself next time you hear: 'Oh, is that what you meant? All this time I've been thinking you meant...'

2. · Insider-speak

Most successful organisations have a language all of their own. Mix up a few of the chairman's favourite phrases, a hefty dose of TLAs (three letter acronyms), and a sprinkling of MBA speak, and what you have is a recipe for confusion. Along comes some keen newcomer eager to suck up the prevailing corporate culture and pretty soon he or she is mimicking the local lingo too. What you have is a cocktail of language that makes sense to those in the know but not to outsiders. And yet ultimately it's always outsiders we are selling to.

The effect of this corporate-speak is slowly and subtly to disconnect the people on the inside (you) from the people on the outside (your customers). The more disconnected you become, the harder it is for you to empathise with your market and recognise new insights. Realness forces you to communicate in the same way as your consumers. It reconnects you with their world.

3 · Brain styles

Finally, not everyone 'gets' information the same way. Research in the field of Neuro-Linguistic Programming (NLP) has shown that people can be divided roughly into three sensory types: auditory, visual and kinesthetic. This means they have a bias to taking in and understanding information using words, pictures or actions respectively. Bias towards each of these three styles is split roughly equally within the adult population. So if your communication at work is based solely on words, then you're only using the favoured medium of a third of your audience. A third would have 'got it better' if you had literally painted a picture, another third would have understood better if you'd got them to act out or try the experience.

TLA mania

A sure sign that you've got your own corporate language is the dreaded three-letter acronym. TLAs are part of a corporate obsession with reducing everything to computer-like code. Your job title, meeting, part of building, market category – even your name is not safe from a corporate attack of the TLAs.

Have you ever received one of these?

To :   MK
From: BN
Cc: HC/OL
Re: MRS and GPR Q3
Please note, this meeting will be held in MR3. Also, due to FUF the NAM will not be present. OL to brief outside the meeting. Thanks.
Brian.

What's happening here? Brian Nicholson is sending a memo to Mike King, and Henry Cooke and Oliver Laurence are copied. The memo invites them to hear a summary of market research (MRS) and a review of gross profit (GPR) made in July, August and September. Brian also asks Oliver to brief the national accounts manager, who is preoccupied with the first updated forecast. It's a brief message and it's efficient – perfect for the ER world – but too much of it and we start speaking and thinking in TLAs. And our customers don't!

The results of a words-only zone

You can begin to see the limitations of using words around creativity. But the penny has yet to drop in most businesses. Instead, verbal cleverness has become in many cases more important than the quality of the content.

'In most companies, people are rewarded for talking – and the longer, the louder, and the more confusingly, the better,' observe Jeffrey Pfeffer and Robert Sutton in an article published in the *Harvard Business Review* June 1999.They call this phenomenon 'Smart Talk' and it results in the 'Smart-Talk Trap'.

'Rare is the manager who presents a new strategy with a single slide and an idea that can be summarised in a sentence,' note Pfeffer and Sutton. Rarer still is the manager who produces a prototype of an idea and lets it do the talking for him. In the corporate environment, managerial ability is often judged by the ability to talk smart, rather than by actually making things happen.

Sounding clever often involves being critical. (Interestingly, research suggests that people who take a negative stance often appear to be brighter than those who are positive.) This has a particularly insidious effect on innovation. The way companies are organised encourages bright people to apply their considerable intellects to sounding clever – and picking holes in everyone else's ideas. The result, say Pfeffer and Sutton, is companies that are 'filled with clever putdown artists' and '...paralysed by the fear and silence these people spawn.'

What can realness do for creativity?

So far we've explored how 'word-only zones' can block creative behaviour. Now let's look at the other side of the coin: what realness can do for creativity. Once you unleash realness in your workplace, its natural affinity with creativity will become crystal clear. Believe us, once you try it you will never go back! But rather than asking you to take our word for it, we have outlined below the three core benefits that realness can bring to creativity at work.

1 · Realness: the idea builder

We've already seen why words are not the best medium for explaining ideas to others in a way that ensures they really get it. When an idea starts to look like the 'real thing', it will evoke reactions that a written concept could not. The minute you get to play with something, new ideas come tumbling out. 'I love it but it's bulkier than I thought it would be.' 'It tastes great but at the price we're talking about there's not enough of it.' 'Ooh, I'm disappointed, I imagined something else.' 'It's really cute – I just love it so much more than I thought I would!'

What's happening here? The prototype gets us feeling and speaking like consumers. We immediately start building and growing the idea in a way that we would not have been able to do unless we actually interacted with it in person. It forces us to examine previously unimagined details. This is important because with innovation, the devil is in the detail. Many a fine idea has failed because the product or service was just that little bit too big, slow, dull, expensive, or had some other obvious shortcoming that could have been rectified if it had been spotted sooner.

Effectively what prototyping does is give you a rich source of fresh insights to go away with and incorporate into your next prototype to drive the project forward.

2 · Realness: the momentum maker

The second way that realness benefits creativity is through momentum. As you will have gathered, the behaviour of realness is not for idle souls! In the next section we will explore the impact momentum has on innovation in detail. For now, just remember this point: prototyping is the equivalent of putting a stick of dynamite down your corporate pants! Sit back and wait for the reaction.

Once something begins to look real, it prompts comment from all parts of the organisation. People wake up and smell the reality. If it falls to them to make these ideas happen, their contribution to the innovation process increases. Where once there was endless discussion, there now will be action. That action may even include saying: 'No, the idea is not worth pursuing, let's stop the project now.' But having the courage to stop is just as important as accelerating innovation projects. Realness pushes you into action in one or other direction, and either way is better than apathy.

Organisations with realness are inclusive organisations. Instead of ideas digitally reduced to bullet point presentations hidden away somewhere in a server, they are out in the open. Real things are ready and waiting for the Chairman, the cleaner, the secretary, the new graduate and the production manager to pick up and literally get a feel of. Whereas beforehand your colleagues had no real idea what it is that you did, now they are banging on your door to share their comments or even join the team.

Black and Decker Paintmate

What would you get if you combined a vacuum cleaner, a garden hose, a two-litre cola bottle and a paintbrush? The answer is the first prototype of the Black and Decker Paintmate, an automatic paint system that feeds paint to the brush, and one of the world's biggest DIY launches. The original prototype proved to the team that the basic idea was sound and encouraged others to step in and support the venture.

3 · Realness: the emotional engager

We are going to make this section real by referring to the cult sci-fi story, *Star Trek*. So if you are not familiar with the original TV series grab your parent, child or neighbour and ask them about the creative behaviour of Captain Kirk and Mr Spock. No doubt they will tell you about Spock's cold calculating logic and of Kirk's remarkable ability to run on gut feelings, of his emotional side, and his bravery. They may also tell you that the two of them made a great pair, very different but complementary.

We see a parallel in creativity. Put simply, Mr Spock would revel in ER situations – he is the RAIN master! – whereas Captain Kirk would thrive in the greenhouse. The thing about Kirk is that he is not afraid to show his feelings. His judgements come from an emotional place deep within him – something Spock frequently finds hard to fathom.

It is this openness about feelings, especially when you can't explain why, that defines really successful innovation cultures. Think about it.

Consumers don't always do things for logical reasons – they often make Kirk not Spock decisions.

Why did Volkswagen bring back the Beetle? Not because the 'Love Bug' is the best car in the world, but because as consumers we love the shape – and probably watched too many Herbie movies in our youth. But at work we often feel inhibited about revealing the Kirk inside us. Work is a place where Spock behaviour is approved of and Kirk behaviour often suppressed. The point is that creativity and the greenhouse operate on gut feel and emotional response. Spock can always shoot down a great but not fully formed idea.

Outside of work, we're all consumers. We live in the 'real world', too. We have hobbies and passions that are reserved for leisure time. Many people find that the more ER-like work becomes, the more important non-ER activity outside of work is to them. The more you bury your head in the spreadsheet, the more you want to garden at the weekend.

Given a chance, many of us like to cook, chop trees, refurbish the loft or make things with our hands. This hands-on thing is missing from most people's professional lives. To be encouraged to do it at work is highly fulfilling. Realness allows people to bring their Kirk persona into work. Suddenly, business is using the 'whole person'. It's literally 'hands-on' – and it's great fun.

> *"Dear friend, theory is all grey, and the golden tree of life is green."*
>
> JOHANN WOLFGANG VON GOETHE
> (1749–1832)

A real environment

Many work environments are unwittingly designed to prevent realness. Everything is fixed – once the computer cabling is in place and the phone system installed there is little scope to change how rooms are used. Everything is expensive – ever bought office furniture? The cost will make you weep! After spending so much on such impersonal kit, it's hard to get messy with paint, glue and cardboard. Many office environments are designed by committee, bought out of a brochure or just not designed at all. Sometimes the office move is delegated to someone with the aesthetic powers of a winkle. We rarely come across office design where the ability to play, to change things or to get rapid access to customers is a factor. Of course there are many exceptions but as far as office design is concerned real life and real play, it seems, are put on hold.

Watch out for the next big leap in office design: domestic offices which reflect the way we live and give us room to play. It's already started. Take British Airways' £200 million shopping mall-style business centre at Waterside near Heathrow, complete with high street, pavement cafés, florist, library and supermarket.

So take a look: how much realness do you have around you?

Making realness happen

Realness is not a sophisticated science; it's more a mindset. Remember the simple mantra: 'How can I make this real now?' Below are our top six insights and observations on making realness real.

1 · Looping the loop

At ?What If!, we use the word 'prototyping' interchangeably with realness. For us, the beauty of prototyping is the unique role it plays in the creative process. Prototyping is not something you do at the end of a creative process, but is an integral part of that process. A common misconception is that making things real is the responsibility of a small group of people in an organisation, say product development. For prototyping read 'learning and inspiring by doing' – a skill we can all adopt, not something that marketing people hand over to implementation people. This misses the value of that all-important question, 'How can we make this real now?'

Prototyping means you quickly turn an idea – words and thoughts – into something real. A prototype is something you can touch, put in your pocket, play with in your hands. You can literally weigh it up. Prototypes are a fantastic way of evolving new insights and builds, and of checking what works and what doesn't. As soon as one prototype is finished and has been interrogated, a new one can be started. Skilled inventors know that the critical issue is how many of these loops they can pack in before launch. This means always asking this question early in the process: 'How can we make it real now?' But also following it up with a, 'Quick, let's incorporate those insights and make it real again.'

The loop

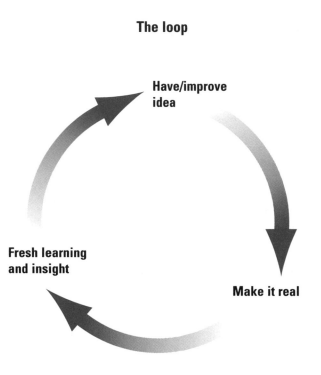

Have/improve idea

Make it real

Fresh learning and insight

The point is that the real value comes from looping the loop. Using the experience and energy of one loop to drive the next. What's more, it's an incredibly exciting and creative behaviour, challenging you to find new approaches and answers.

> *"If a picture is worth a thousand words, then a prototype is worth a million."*
> TREVOR BAYLIS, INVENTOR OF THE CLOCKWORK RADIO

Dyson – 5127 loops

Today, James Dyson is regarded as one of Britain's leading entrepreneurs and inventors. The story of his 'dual cyclone' vacuum cleaner is the stuff of business legend. Dyson beat near bankruptcy to establish his factory in Malmesbury, Wiltshire, and become the UK market leader. Throughout it all, he has never lost sight of the importance of realness.

Dyson invented the bagless 'dual cyclone' vacuum cleaner in 1978, back when flared trousers were in fashion (the first time round). Like most overnight successes, it's been a long journey. Five long years and 5127 prototypes later, his idea became a working model. But it was another ten years before the product reached the market.

In between, Dyson tried unsuccessfully to get backing from the leading manufacturers. It was an eye-opening introduction to the world of big business. His brush with the corporate world gave him important insights into the sort of management culture that prevailed in some large companies. He was determined that his own firm would be different.

When he finally launched in 1993, Dyson's first product, the DC01, turned the UK market for upright cleaners on its head. Just 23 months after its launch, his invention became Britain's best-selling vacuum cleaner, overtaking sales of Hoover, Electrolux, Panasonic and Miele. It was followed in 1995 by the DC02, the company's cylinder cleaner, which achieved similar results.

Today, the distinctive yellow, grey and purple vacuum cleaners are to be found in homes the length and breadth of the country. Dyson remains wary of the corporate mindset, and ensures the company culture also stands out from the crowd. Memos are banned, because he says they are 'just a way of passing the buck'. He has an even lower opinion of e-mail: 'The graphics are so appalling I just can't get interested enough to read them,' he says.

Company employees must follow two rules: no smoking and no ties. (When he was trying to get financial backing for his invention, Dyson once told the board of a company on America's East Coast that ties make you go deaf in your old age.)

A hands-on familiarity with the product, the company believes, means that employees are passionate. Every new employee – including a former Trade Minister, Richard Needham, when he joined the company as a non-executive director – spends the first day assembling one of the famous dual cyclone machines. They can then buy the fruits of their own labour for £20 and take it home for their own use.

Individuality is also a strong feature of the company's culture. The company has a slogan: 'We should be human beings not business people.' Many staff are recruited straight from university because their minds are open to new ideas and working methods.

They are encouraged to be different as a matter of principle – it's part of what James Dyson calls his 'anti-brilliance campaign'. 'Very few people can be brilliant,' he says. 'And they are overvalued. It's much more exciting to be a pioneer. Be a bit whacko and you shake people up. We all need shaking up.'*

*Dearlove, Des, 'Long road to a big clean-up', The Times, 30 July 1998.

2 · Realness knows no limits

There are some forms of realness that are more apparent than others. We can all see how to mock-up a new product but what about a service, or a meeting, or a conversation, or an internal process? Realness is just as applicable to services as to products. It's just that the methods may vary.

Take financial services, for instance. You don't buy much of a 'thing', just benefits. You can't 'make' a new type of home mortgage. Or can you? We believe there is always a way. The key is to put yourself in consumers' shoes. Actors call this rehearsal or role play – the chance to experiment or explore something in real life not in words.

Let's imagine you are trying to prototype an innovative home mortgage. Why not mock up an advert for the mortgage and slip it into an appropriate magazine? Leave your colleagues to discover it. Or why not drill some independent financial advisors in the benefits of your home loan idea and have them role play trying to make some sales? This isn't market research. It's getting a close approximation of your idea out into the real world, instead of allowing it to languish on paper in a filing cabinet.

Some products are simple but rely on a complex ritual of use and appreciation. In these cases, there is all the more need to prototype, especially if the end-user is very different to you. At ?What If!, we often ask our clients to act out or role play their brands rather than just talk to us about them. Try this; it works. Ask the members of your team to come to your next development meeting with a picture of someone from your target market pulled from a magazine. Then get them to introduce themselves as this person and tell the team about their life. Question them, too. Make sure they stick to the first person narrative. Ask them to give their opinion on your particular product development.

You will be amazed at the richness of information they provide. They'll tell you things that are all too easy to discount as unimportant when you are wrapped up in the corporate world. Remember, it's only a prototype, don't worry about whether what they say is completely accurate. What counts is that they stimulate you to consider product improvements. The beauty of this prototyping is that it can be used to bring anything to life. For the courier example below we could easily have applied the same principles to prototyping a new internal distribution system, a new management development review process, or any other internal process re-engineering initiative.

Delivering some realness

Some services are complex in their delivery. For instance, take the new wave of courier tracking systems that have been launched. Perhaps the big idea is to tell customers where their goods are, using a pre-recorded message that telephones them to say where the parcel is in its journey. How would you prototype this?

You could find a large room, plenty of willing volunteers and turn your ideas into a mini play. Each volunteer could play the role of a part of the value chain. So someone could be the executive who wants to send a package; someone else the PA making the arrangements; someone else the courier company telephonist who takes the order; and so on. Don't worry, you won't need the talents of Steven Spielberg to direct this production. In fact, why not run several versions of the play? You could give each version a title or scenario such as: 'Happy Customer'; 'Technology Failure'; 'Budget Version'; 'Spot the Difference from the Competition'; and so on. The very act of walking through – in this case, acting through – each stage of the process and each scenario will force you to focus on the details of the idea.

The question is always the same and repeats like a mantra in the head of the inventor: 'How can I make it real right now?' Always ask yourself this question of your creative tasks.

Realness challenge

1 · **What if you made it real with a video?**
2 · **What if you made it real with a radio play?**
3 · **What if you made it real on a huge picture – the size of your biggest office wall?**
4 · **What if you made it real by banning words and numbers?**
5 · **What if you made it real by buying the next best thing from a customer perspective?**
6 · **What if you made it real by getting customers to draw what they wanted?**
7 · **What if you made it real by having your customer's environment in your offices?**
8 · **What if you made it real by moving your office to the customer's environment?**
9 · **What if you made it real every day?**
10 · **What if you all made it real in secret and then showed each other?**
11 · **What if you made it real in 24 hours?**
12 · **What if…**

3 · Realness in action

Realness is a powerful tool for creative internal change as well as for product and service innovation. If you have an idea for changing how things are at work, get on and 'make it real now'.

One of the most common areas for internal innovation is communicating more effectively. If you have an idea about a new type of meeting, don't wait to get agreement from all parties (you won't), just try it out. (Some of our experiments with meetings are described in the next chapter.)

If you want to get a feel early on in a project's life about what top management will say, why not pretend you are the Board. Get someone to act out how the finance director will react, what the CEO will say and so on. The issue is the same – let's stop talking and make the experience real now.

4 · Encourage imperfection

Never forsake realness for the sake of 'finishedness'. Prototypes are rough and ready. That's part of their magic. They are the best you can do with the time and available resources. If a prototype is too finished, it actually stops people from commenting. If it's that finished, they think, then it's no longer under development.

Your prototypes should shout out, 'Come and change me, don't leave me like this!' Remember that you will loop the loop over and over again with your prototypes. In the previous courier example, if all the participants in the role play know they will produce, say, ten versions of their plays, it will affect how they prototype. They know it's not the final version, so they will happily dive in and give it a go without worrying about making a fool of themselves.

This was brought home to us when we mocked up a completely new holiday brochure in under four hours! Previously, we had shown fully designed dummy brochures to two groups of consumers. We quickly realised that what we thought was a striking new brochure was just more of the same to our audience. So it was back to school time. With pens, crayons, pictures from magazines and scissors and a lot of glue, we cobbled together two very rough, but radically different, designs. The level of finish was no higher than you'd expect from a group of 11-year-olds. But the next two consumer research groups didn't care; they could see and talk about our new ideas, they were excited and could build on what we'd done. The prototypes became the tool through which a whole new direction emerged. It was a striking confirmation of realness rather than an obsession with perfection.

5 · Share your realness

Don't lock your prototypes away – leave them lying about in your office. We guarantee your colleagues and your boss will be drawn to them like a moth to a flame. They'll leave notes on your desk with advice and praise. Even better, your boss will steal your prototype and show it to his or her boss. Before you know it, your innovation project will have attracted attention and will have the heavy guns behind it. And all because you made it real.

Hewlett Packard has made this principle part of its culture. All technical staff are encouraged to have the latest prototype of the project they're

"Chop your own wood –
it will warm you twice."

PROVERB

working on sitting on their desk at all times. Colleagues can see how work is progressing and make comments and suggestions to improve it. The company also recognises that because staff are also consumers, it is a great way to get a consumer reaction as early as possible. It means that HP employees don't think in abstract terms, but physical reality. They live with the product every day, just as the customer will.

6 · Don't think, just leap

We can promise you that the first time you introduce realness at work not everyone will be happy to participate. There are always those who find the path less travelled an uncomfortable route (you know who they are). Do not give up. Just dive in and have a go. This is the very essence of creativity. Just do it. It will be hard at first but the benefits can only be experienced by doing it.

Organising realness

We think that realness will become an increasingly important source of competitive advantage. We've come across a number of companies who already structure realness into the way they work. Here are some examples.

Van den Bergh: your desk in a kitchen

If you work in a food company, shouldn't you work in a kitchen? That was the thought behind Van den Bergh Holland's decision to build a completely new food development facility.

Integrating marketing and R&D, the new facility contains fully functioning kitchens, development laboratories and teaching areas as well as the basic workplace requirements of desks and chairs. Throw into the pot consumer workshops, food demonstrations, cookery courses and visiting chefs, and the company bubbles with realness.

Saatchi & Saatchi: keep clients waiting

London advertising agency Saatchi and Saatchi used realness to great effect in winning the pitch for the British Rail advertising business. Senior rail executives were kept waiting outside the meeting until they reached breaking point and got ready to leave. At this point the team stepped in, explaining that these were the same feelings rail customers felt for the notoriously erratic train service, and went on to deliver advertising which sought to address this issue. Once the nerves had calmed, the business was won.

People's Bank: don't debate it – test it

People's Bank has a refreshingly original attitude to new ideas. 'Don't debate it, test it,' is one of the key philosophies of this innovative American financial services organisation. Fed up with endlessly debating whether an idea was a winner or loser and learning little along the way, the bank shifted its paradigm to a 'test it before you judge it' approach. The result is an organisation dedicated to making new ideas real as quickly as possible then piloting them in managed circumstance to check the appeal and improve the idea.

Next: what's next?

Leading UK fashion retailer Next is renowned for its high quality, simple and innovative shop layouts with each new season of clothes. Probe for the secret of its consistent success and you discover that back at HQ is a full-size mock-up of a high street shop. This way buyers, designers and merchandisers are forced to not just buy the clothes, but look at how the new ranges live and feature in the real shopping environment.

With these sorts of structures you can return to your inventive roots. Rather than feeling frustrated, you can get your hands dirty and start to give life to your ideas.

Realness with consumers

Market research has driven a huge wedge between the consumer and the provider. Ever more complicated techniques mean we spend our time reading reports rather than making consumer experiences real. This isn't to say that we don't value market research. It's just we believe it should be complemented by real experience. (How many of you are your target market?)

Over the last few years we've:
◆ Hired a street for the day to immerse an R&D department in the consumer's world.
◆ Had the board of a company present its five-year plan to consumers.
◆ Been to breakfast with a different family every day of the week.
◆ Had consumers conduct a cost reduction exercise rather than the technical teams.

None of this was meant to replace market research. But what it did was give us the real experience from which to grow and develop our thinking. So next time you look at your research budget consider some consumer realness.

Summary

Realness at work means that you stop talking and sending memos. It means that you ask yourself a simple question: 'How can I make this real right now?'

The aim is to find a way of reproducing the experience you were so busy talking about, and bring the idea to life.

For lots of organisations, this goes against the grain. They have created 'word-only cultures'. Realness involves a revolution in the way we behave at work.

The benefits are better ideas, more momentum and greater fulfilment at work.

Do it early and see how many times you can loop the loop.

Don't be a perfectionist.

Share your prototypes.

Just do it now.

Go on!

momentum

Most people say generating ideas isn't the problem —
it's making them happen that's really hard.

Is this you?

◆ You are a starter not a finisher.

◆ You suffer from death by diary – you hold a brainstorm; it's exciting and the team is buzzing, but when you arrange the follow-up no one can make it for several weeks.

◆ You are so busy being busy that you can't find time to really get stuck into any of your projects.

◆ You feel like you use most of your energy battling with your organisation instead of the competition.

◆ Be honest – it's a long time since you were really passionate about your work.

◆ You are still working on projects that have been floating around the business for ages.

What is momentum?

Have you ever watched kids playing? They have a focus and intensity about them that seems to shut out everything else. The big cardboard box (the one the washing machine came in) is really a boat. The kids are rushing around collecting provisions for their voyage. Interrupt their mission to give them a meal, and they stop just long enough to wolf it down. Then they're off again – back to the boat. Now they're rigging up a sail from a broom handle and an old sheet. There is a focus and happy spontaneity to their play. This is momentum.

Late nights, caffeine and pizza

Most of us can conjure up an image of Bill Gates and his partner Paul Allen battling it out in the early days of Microsoft. Lots of late nights, caffeine, take-out pizza. Did they even notice the time? Probably not. That's what happens when a team is pulling in the same direction. They were on a mission, personally motivated and exhilarated by the same goal. Lots of laughter; lots of setbacks. This, too, is momentum. Momentum is all about getting on and doing whatever you have to do to make something happen. It's not about taking small bites out of a task whenever time permits. It's about really getting your teeth into it; wrestling it to the floor.

How does momentum fit with growth?

The reason momentum plays such a key role in innovation is clear when you break down the innovation process into its three component parts:

Insights + Ideas + Impact = Innovation

We call this the 'Innovation Equation'. It recognises that unless creative ideas are based on a real insight and get to see the commercial light of day (make an impact), they won't benefit the business. They may be great fun, but are little more than entertaining distractions. Momentum connects up these three Is. It's the driving force behind improving ideas and getting on and making them happen. Put simply, momentum underpins the culture of organisations that put creativity to work and turn it into innovation.

What does momentum look like?

Maybe you're a 'Momentum God' already; perhaps you can add to this list? Here's what people with momentum are up to.

◆ *'Instead of swapping e-mails let's meet now and talk.'*

◆ *'Don't write a report for me – just call me on the mobile and we'll make a decision.'*

◆ *'Brief me on your problem, give me an hour to think it through and sketch out a solution for you to respond to. If you like it and we can agree the changes, get on and do it.'*

◆ *'Who really needs to be in this meeting?'*

◆ *''Do we have 70% of the information we need? Then let's do it!'*

◆ *'What's your gut instinct? Why don't we go with that, what's the worst that could happen?'*

◆ *''I know it should take 6 months – but what would we have to do differently to get it done in 3?'*

If your instinctive reaction to these statements is positive, that this is the way business should be, then you're going to love momentum!

What momentum is not

Some people and organisations hide behind a mask of being busy. Make no mistake – momentum is not speed. Speed can be part of momentum, but there's more to it than just doing things quickly. It is helpful to distinguish between 'good energy' momentum, which is vital to innovation, and 'bad energy' momentum, the unplanned urgency and crises associated with ER situations. Momentum is not firefighting or being busy for the sake of it.

Some organisations seem to have perfected the myth that constant twelve-hour days and weekend working are somehow good; but momentum is not about doing lots. It's about creating the time to apply focus and energy. Making momentum happen is a proactive and creative act. But it comes at a cost, something has to give. Momentum is not free.

The effects of 'bad energy' momentum are very evident. At a personal level the stress of unplanned crises is draining and unhealthy. At a corporate level organisations that lurch from one mini crisis to the next and that are full of unfinished projects end up being weak, devoured or dead.

"If at first an idea is not absurd then there is no hope for it."
ALBERT EINSTEIN

Momentum and creativity

Ideas are tender when young. Often what turns out as a great idea was originally thought of as absurd.

In the face of cynicism it takes a strong individual to keep pursuing their 'absurdity', and the longer they take to pursue the idea the less focused they are and the more chance there is for doubt to take hold. 'Perhaps my CEO is right? Perhaps my idea is not so great? Come to think of it it's been a while since I last talked to some consumers about my idea, did they really like it that much?'

Momentum doesn't give the destructive power of self-doubt time to take hold. It carries with it an exuberance that is hard for the cynic to fight. Many people will crush others' ideas, not through considered analysis, but defensive reaction: 'Heck, why didn't I think of that?' Momentum gives us energy, it can make us smile and laugh together – this is a potent force against the defensive cynic, who will think twice before bursting an energy bubble.

Momentum and motivation

There is another important aspect to momentum beyond its role in creativity. Momentum is the behaviour all great growth leaders have. They know that NOW is the time to really push, to forget all other initiatives, and focus. In doing so they are listening to their gut instincts. Think of it as an unreasonable sense of urgency, albeit with a real clarity of direction. Leaders with momentum can be frustrating at times, infuriating even, but life is never dull around them.

> *"Cynics are the mass murderers of ideas and all ideas can be murdered."*
> DR CURTIS CARLSON,
> CEO, SRI INTERNATIONAL (FORMERLY STANFORD RESEARCH INSTITUTE)

Skilled innovators instinctively know how to create this state. They know that there will be times when the motivation and energy of their team will be at odds with the direction of their organisation. The whole point about innovation is that it is unpredictable and organisations just aren't set up to deal with the unpredictable. Innovation projects uncover uncomfortable truths. For instance, the new manufacturing plant is not appropriate to produce the great new idea – how painful then to shift the company to looking at outside supply! The innovation project team is motivated by outside supply but the company wants it in-house. The innovation director knows that this is a critical point in time when they have to act and act fast. He or she alone can now create momentum by giving the team the permission to explore beyond the existing corporate manufacturing strategy and look into an exciting new world of outside supply. This is how momentum is created – by allowing people to do what their gut tells them to do, what they think is right. This is enormously liberating. The alternative is that the innovation director keeps his or her head in the sand and ignores the value of harnessing others' energy.

Examples of how momentum can be created by leaders

◆ *'Hang on a minute, isn't your time better spent on this project? Don't worry about that report, the world will keep turning.'*

◆ *'Show me your diary, I'm going to help you find time to do this project properly.'*

◆ *'From now on I want a verbal briefing every morning – no presentations, just tell me where we're up to.'*

◆ *'I know this new project means you have to shift priorities at work. Don't worry we'll alter your bonus criteria to match.'*

◆ *'Can we decide this without discussing it?'*

◆ *'Don't come into the office, work from home!'*

◆ *'Let's divide this task up and crack it between us.'*

But momentum is not just for leaders. The ability to know when and where to focus, to pick your battle, is one that marks out people at all levels who are effective at getting things done. To us, momentum is the management of human energy. The trouble is, most managers don't consciously manage this aspect of their work. 'Energy management' is understood at an intuitive level, and practised instinctively. But it is not yet recognised as a legitimate business skill. It's not something that's discussed, so it remains in the background of business life.

Losing momentum – the danger signs

1 · Lack of belief

Inspiring individuals to contribute innovative ideas on a regular basis goes hand-in-hand with demonstrating momentum. If you believe your company will make it happen, you are far more likely to contribute your creativity to the innovation process. But without careful management, the dark forces of inertia within a company can take hold. Pretty soon it becomes part of the corporate mythology that the Board will not take risks. This is something we find perplexing as we are often briefed by senior managers who complain that junior staff do not present them with provocative plans.

Inertia is the arch-enemy of momentum. If an innovation project is worth doing, do it with momentum.

2 · Growth without energy management

In a small business, maintaining momentum is much easier. There are fewer people to create bottlenecks, fewer systems to get in the way, less need for planning. Often these businesses have that magical 'start up' energy and an attitude that anything is possible: 'Let's just give it a go.'

But as companies become bigger they begin to lose these energising momentum factors, often without realising it. Systems can all too easily get out of control and start to take over. What was once a coffee machine huddle is now an extended and bureaucratic approval process. There are so many people to keep in the loop that innovation leaders spend more time making sure that everyone is informed (or 'covered off') than actually having new ideas and driving projects. As businesses grow they hunger for predictability. The bigger they get, the hungrier they become. With size and success comes responsibility to shareholders and staff. It's natural then that big business wants to plan and manage the future as precisely as the clock ticks a new day.

Unfortunately, momentum doesn't fit neatly into this scheme of things. It upsets the predictable beat of the planner's clock. By its very nature momentum behaviour is often unplanned. It demands that we follow where our passion leads us. We only really know how hard to push once a project is in motion. You can't plan it in advance.

These three factors then – the growth of systems, increasing numbers of people and the demands for planning – can have an enormously negative effect on your organisation's ability to keep up momentum. We wouldn't be surprised if you had predicted all three factors. However, there is a repercussion that receives very little attention: the deliberate management of energy and emotion. This again is a factor of growth. Big business finds it hard to maintain an intimate (almost family) feel. The common spirit and passion that binds a small group of people together is replaced by a salary structure and a promotion system. Over time, these competitive arenas become the last place people show their emotions.

Most managers are not aware of how to recognise when momentum is needed and feel uneasy about 'managing' someone else's energy or emotion. (We use the words emotion and energy interchangeably here, as the former drives the latter.) This comes from a fear that, in confronting the emotional aspects of work, we may reveal too much about ourselves, or intrude on the private lives of others. It's easier to hide behind a mask of professionalism.

At the moment, lots of potential 'energy managers' out there feel that work is work – a place to get the job done. After work, they tell themselves, we are free to be who we really want to be. So why interfere? This is fine up to a point, but it creates an obstacle to introducing creativity and innovation into the workplace.

The myth that business isn't meant to be fun, that good business is serious business, has done more to suppress momentum than any other single factor. We started this section with a reference to kids playing – there are many who find other people's enthusiasm at work 'childish'. We reject this notion. Emotion, enthusiasm, energy, passion, whatever you want to call it, is the lifeblood of innovation.

3 · Underestimating the innovation roller-coaster

Asking people at work to be productively creative, to be innovative, is to ask them to do a fundamentally difficult job. What we mean by asking someone to take the job of innovation director is to ask them to challenge the system, try new things – and expensive, risky ones at that.

The innovation director won't have a lot of ammunition to take up the good fight with. He will often have to argue from a position of gut feel, not fact (Kirk not Spock), have little resource and be surrounded by a mixed audience, some open and some cynical. Perhaps life is kinder to innovators in your organisation – if so, you are exceptional. The barriers most innovation directors will experience will not be apparent at the start of an innovation project. Starting a project is like rolling a ball downhill. People love to escape the ER environment for a while and let their hair down in the greenhouse. Creative sessions are a welcome break from almost any job. People revel in their new-found freedom to challenge accepted wisdom. These are the heady early days of an innovation project when anything seems possible.

The honeymoon period doesn't last long. The reality is that there are a lot of knocks in store along the way. The almost naively optimistic energy of the initial stage can go one of two ways depending on the skill of the leader. Either it will begin to falter and eventually stall or it will become like a freight train.

Here are ten examples of the uphill stages of an innovation roller-coaster.

1. *At the end of the creative session someone takes the notes to type up.
   Three weeks later, when you eventually see them, they communicate none
   of the excitement you felt at the meeting. In fact you wonder if they are
   the notes from the same meeting.*

2. *Halfway through a project, trading conditions dictate that only a fraction
   of funds promised are available to support the launch.*

3. *Your technical colleagues shake their heads and say, 'Sorry we've
   changed our minds, we can't make it to the original spec.'*

4. *Your project never seems to be the first thing on your list of urgent things
   to do.*

5. *The new finance director asks for facts about how much of this new idea
   you will sell.*

6. *The Board suffers collective memory loss, and forgets why it was a good
   idea in the first place.*

7. *Your team don't call you anymore to tell you what they think you should
   do next.*

8. *Your boss leaves.*

9. *You hear that a competitor is about to launch the same thing.*

10. Your partner calls you when you are working late again, and they are not impressed with your excuses about the importance of momentum. Your dinner ends up in the dog.

Fast-moving new hair products for Black African consumers

Unilever in South Africa had been trying to get into the afro hair care market for nearly 15 years with no success. Then in a last ditch attempt a crack team was set up. Their mission was to make a huge success where nobody else had succeeded and make the impossible possible. Their publicly stated aim was to become famous in Unilever for doing so! This vision inspired everyone involved; they could do it. They threw themselves at the project, having regular one- and two-day workshops, going on lots of 'consumer and stylist safaris', and even having their hair 'relaxed', (a process where an uncomfortable burning product was applied to their hair to straighten it). In short, anything they needed to do to get a winning product to market.

Throughout the process the momentum was infectious; research agencies used to doing at least half a dozen groups were debriefing after only one. 'We were always working with only 60% knowledge, but if we believed we were on the right lines, we would go on to the next stage. The energy was unbelievable,' said the project leader Kathy Tucker.

4 · Bar coding time

'Bar coding' time is the great management disabler of our age, and we're all guilty of it to a greater or lesser extent. It involves the habit of managing as many things as you can in a day, working in hourly chunks (sometimes even smaller) without ever really having the time to focus on one project with any real intensity.

What we do is slice the working day into as many slivers of time as possible and use them to cover as many tasks as we can. You can imagine looking at a busy manager's diary and seeing a bar code! Managers are spreading themselves too thinly in a desperate attempt to do too much. The effect is that they don't ever give a decent push to any one project. Is your diary a bar code diary?

A day in our working life   stop, start, stop, start...

Most time management systems seem to pander to this. They focus on helping the modern manager to juggle as many activities in one business day as is humanly possible. (And haven't we become good at it!)

Bar coding time kills creativity. You may feel fantastic because you have managed to keep so many balls in the air, but creativity requires more, it needs a passion for the subject. Lots of short meetings mean you have to fall in love with your task all over again every time you come back to it.

In this way bar coding time drains the build-up of momentum and siphons off enthusiasm. The original passion for the project may be rediscovered towards the middle or end of each mini session, but it's lost by the time of the next session. Time is wasted getting momentum back again. Contrary to popular belief, at work absence does not make the heart grow fonder, it just makes it forget.

How many times have you heard or said yourself, 'Hurry up, let's finish the agenda, I've got a train to catch.' Momentum thrives on the kind of energy created when people have a get-together and relax. They need to toy with new ideas, to let the forces of serendipity work their magic and weave their spell. Shooting the breeze is a legitimate innovation tool!

Is it any wonder so many of the executives we talk to speak of a soulless existence at work? Bar coding time misses the point about how humans invent. We work best when we pursue our passion.

In the spirit of momentum, let's move swiftly on and look at how momentum is made.

Making momentum

1 · Seek alignment

The primary thing that drives momentum is alignment. Before you embark on a voyage of innovation, check whether you have it or not. Ensure all participants want the same thing.

Chaos kicks in when people's motivations are not aligned with those of their projects. At some point in the innovation process someone will crack under the pressure and think: 'No, I don't want to do this enough to keep working so hard.' They may tell you this or they may keep it to themselves. Working at half throttle, not willing to take risks or to go the extra mile, these people may put on a pretence of momentum, but their heart isn't in it. (They are not always easy to spot.)

The result of this misalignment is confused or even chaotic energy, rather than aligned energy. The sensation can be likened to a misfiring engine. It isn't like the smooth purr of human horsepower that comes with alignment. You find yourself devoting more time to looking out for members of the team who are either not interested or not performing. Perhaps you feel you spend more time on your 'bad' people than 'good' people? The result is a gradual falling off of momentum as the forces of inertia take hold, and eventually the project stalls.

Spotting cracks in alignment

1. *Your project team can't agree on why their work is so important – there's no clarity around the insight behind the project.*

2. *Some of your team, while they were enthusiastic to begin with, seem to have lost their power to 'self-start'.*

3. *You hear about initiatives sanctioned by the Board that seem to be at odds with what you thought were your project's goals.*

4. *Privately, some members of your project team complain to you about other members. Why are they on the team? What added value do they bring?*

5. *You don't look forward to team meetings.*

Momentum making alignment

1. *Everyone knows what judgement criteria will be used to assess the project.*

2. *They understand how the project fits in to the company's wider strategic objectives – team members can easily gauge its importance.*

3. *Everyone knows how important the project is compared to all the other work they have to do – they can prioritise for themselves.*

4. *The focus is on achieving the goals – not internal politics (outfighting not infighting).*

5. Your team feels 'together' and supportive – they're buzzing.

6. The members of your team don't just understand the objective itself, they understand the intent. They can answer the question: 'Why are we doing this?' They can answer it straight away and without any prompting.

Momentum at *Metro*

Metro is the world's largest free morning newspaper. It's the morning diet of nearly a million commuters coming into London or seven other major cities in the UK. In 2001 it was the Marketing Society's brand of the year and its advertising rates are nearly double the average national newspaper rate. Advertisers pay more to advertise in *Metro* to communicate with ABC1 adults under 35 than any other newspaper in the country. Impressed? You should be – most of Britain's newspapers have been around since radios were called 'wirelesses' and yet *Metro* has achieved all this before its third birthday.

Metro's momentum started in mid-1999 when Mike Anderson was called in by Associated Newspapers to rescue their four-month-old fledgling paper. Despite its novel looks (it's smaller than most papers and stapled), *Metro* was struggling to find a niche. Mike decided to get out of the office and on the road and really get a taste of his market. He was standing at the mouth of the 'Drain' (London's Waterloo station escalators disgorge and suck in hundreds of thousands of tired commuters every day) when the realisation hit him; this was a newspaperman's dream – prosperous and purposeful people engaged in a mind-numbingly boring commute – and thousands of them. Most importantly they had nothing to read, nothing new to look at. As Mike puts it: 'At that moment I knew we had something unbelievable.'

Soon Mike had the Associated Newspapers Board out of the boardroom and into the Drain with him. With their excitement and agreement they set about revolutionising the newspaper industry. Mike and his team christened what they had seen as the 'Metro Moment' and branded his audience 'Urbanites' – minds that are fresh and uncluttered, super-receptive to advertising. Advertising rates were increased seven-fold (yes, we said X7!) and yet revenues increased! Everybody wanted to be part of the *Metro* Moment.

The great thing about *Metro*'s story is that they didn't research these changes, they just got on and made them happen. Alignment and belief drove Mike Anderson's team to do what they knew to be right and do it quickly. Today *Metro* is a buzzing, happy crew, proud of their culture and very much on the front foot ready to wrestle their next initiative to the ground.

2 · Create crisis

Have you ever tried to put a presentation together against the clock? You can almost guarantee a catalogue of disasters. First the printer runs out of ink, then the photocopier jams and of course you discover half the pages have been bound upside down. Sound familiar? What happens next? People rally round. They drop what they are doing and muck in. Somehow it all gets sorted in the end. You rush off with perfect documents, thanking everyone profusely whilst cursing the photocopier.

In those few precious minutes of photocopier hell there was perfect alignment. Your goal was the same as everyone else's. There was no time for politics or debate, only one thing mattered.

Sometimes you can create a crisis to provoke alignment – but only when the deadlines are real. Too often businesses cry wolf, expecting people to drive projects forward to meet deadlines that have little real meaning. You can't spend all your time in crisis. You need the rest and space that comes with comfort. But as a short-term way to create momentum, crisis can be highly effective.

Here are a couple of, 'create a crisis', stories but be warned: there are only so many times you can create a burning platform before people refuse to jump!

Virgin's cola crisis

Virgin Cola grew out of the development of a premium cola formula by a Canadian company called Cott. Cott had come to the UK in the mid 1990s and had already launched a number of own-label cola brands for supermarket chains such as Safeway. The company was interested in launching a branded cola, so it approached Virgin's Richard Branson.

Branson and a member of his design team met with the company and were interested in the idea. They mocked up a few cans to see how they looked. After discussion with only a few employees, the Virgin Chairman decided to go ahead. His main concern was the level of come-back that Pepsi and Coca-Cola would be able to afford to mount. Against these two giants, he believed his only chance of getting ahead was to take them by surprise. That way they wouldn't have time to put big defensive plans in place.

In the UK, he went on News at Ten, ITN's flagship television news programme, to announce to the world his intention to launch a cola in just eight weeks' time, despite never having made a drink before. At that moment, no more than a handful of Virgin employees had any clue about his plans. So it came as just as much of a surprise to them as it was to the competition.

By creating a 'crisis', Branson forced his people to be very creative about the launch. The momentum was generated by the need for speed and the cola was somehow launched within the seemingly impossible eight-week window.

A little white lie!

A large multinational confectionery and drinks company asked us to help its sales managers identify new promotional activities. We organised a brainstorming session in the backroom of a local pub to greenhouse ideas. The participating managers duly arrived armed with a list of ideas they felt had real potential to move the business forward.

We developed some of these and then moved into the next phase: time-tabling the actions. The managers found it hard to make the time to keep up the momentum on the projects. All complained that they were already heavily committed. Diaries were consulted. Excuses made. Regret expressed. But despite much cajoling from us, the schedule they came up with was pretty undemanding. Spread over the next 12 months, the projects had little chance of catching fire, and would probably wither and die.

At the next session we disingenuously introduced a new incentive. We cooked up a story about a fax from a competitor that had been found in the car park of a supermarket chain, one of their leading customers. We persuaded their boss to play along and to tell them that the competitor was working on some similar initiatives and had ambitious plans to launch its new product range within six months. Suddenly the atmosphere in the room changed. A number of those present suspected it was a put-up job, but one manager in particular responded in deadly earnest. His reaction was infectious. The managers now responded to what they saw as a competitive threat.

Diaries were reconsulted. Excuses were brushed aside. Regret was transformed into enthusiasm. After some discussion, they concluded that there was, after all, some space to move the schedule forward. They could mobilise their resources to get the ideas actioned, no problem!

Once the challenge was set before them, they rose to it magnificently. The point of this story isn't to criticise these managers or their company. Rather, the story serves to illustrate what happens all the time. Innovation is seen as a long-term pay-off, when it should be seen as the key to competitive position. As a result, it is hard to get people to make space to create momentum and beat the competition to the punch.

3 · Just say no!

There is nothing new in saying, 'Do less'. 'Less breadth, more depth' is a common message most of us have heard, agreed with, and often spectacularly failed at. 'Put the big rocks in the jar first,' goes the time management story. Our time is of course limited; there is only so much time you can put in a jar! If you fill the jar with all the little rocks first there will be no room for the big ones later. It's pretty obvious. But there's a big difference between common sense and common practise.

Why do so few of us manage to focus on just the big rocks? Our observation is that most of us don't take the time to pause and really sort out the big rocks (the important projects) from the small ('nice to do' but potential time wasters). Instead, we accept that they are all big – we view everything we're working on as vital.

How can we tell which are genuinely small rocks, the ones we could relatively easily discard with no real impact on the business or our own goals? To answer this question we need to figure out what we really want to get out of life at work. Looking into ourselves and identifying what is and isn't important involves a degree of introspection that we are not used to in work situations. Most people aren't even aware they need to do it. Moreover there is real pain in choosing to focus on some projects over others. We'd all like to do everything and we can't – the jar has limited capacity. Saying 'no' to some projects hurts. But we've observed that successful innovators have a ruthless streak – they know how to say 'no'.

If you can't say 'no', then take our tip – get some help! The power of a fresh mind, not entangled with suffocating detail, makes tough decisions much easier as the stories below illustrate.

Saying 'No' at Apple

When Steve Jobs returned to Apple as CEO he was shocked to find so many diverse projects underway. He decided to rationalise – to say 'no' to some projects. With Jobs back in charge, Apple narrowed its focus to just two types of computer user – the professional and the home user – and focused its firepower on two types of hardware – desktop and mobile.

This meant the company effectively had only four projects to work on. The pain of this decision was to effectively cut out plenty of potentially lucrative markets. So was the pain worth it? The first result of Apple's new-found focus was the fantastically successful iMac. Apple out-smarted the competition by bringing out a computer that not only had the Mac's legendary user-friendliness, but also looked completely different from all preceding computers. What was the secret of Apple's success? Fewer projects meant that senior management could get much more involved in the detail of the ideas and decisions could be turned around in hours not weeks.

Saying 'No' at Sun

Co-founder of Sun Microsystems Bill Joy has been described as the Edison of the Internet. *Fortune* magazine noted that he was on a '20-year streak of innovation that has laid the groundwork for a new technological era'.

While still a student he shaped AT&T's Unix operating system. He's also credited with designing the most crucial circuits in Sun's SPARC microprocessor, which drives the company's work stations and servers. But it is for masterminding the transformation of obscure programming language into a software phenomenon, Java, that he is perhaps best known. That might never have happened without a conscious decision to focus on fewer projects.

Throughout the 1980s, Joy took on more and more responsibility at Sun, becoming chief scientist and director of technology. Despite his accomplishments some aspects of the job began to niggle him. In particular he spent too much time meeting budgets, in meetings where he wasn't needed, approving or killing projects, and refereeing turf wars.

By the end of the 1980s, the volume of projects he was involved with and the intensity of working in Silicon Valley made him hunger for a change of scene. After a brief spell in San Francisco, Joy moved to Aspen, Colorado. There he was able to minimise his direct reports and follow his whims.

The move was not without some risk. The danger was that, by moving his small research team away from the 'action', he would lose touch with the decision-makers back in Silicon Valley. But he decided the change was worth it.

'I concluded that you're best off away from the action sometimes,' he recalls. 'It was sort of like, "do you rule in hell or serve in heaven?"'

Out in Aspen, Joy had time to really focus on the technology. A project called Oak had been developed to support interactive TV which hadn't materialised. It was ahead of its time, but he could see its potential.

The change of scene in Aspen gave him the opportunity to focus on the language he thought could be the future of the Internet, and which became Java. The rest, as they say, is history.

As Sun's CEO Scott McNealy puts it, 'AT&T has Bell labs, and we have Bill Joy. We get a lot more for our money.'

Let's look at one of the greatest devourers of a manager's time – meetings. Some of our clients estimate that they spend as much as 75% of their time in meetings, only half of which are judged to be truly productive.

Have you ever sorted through all your clothes and surprised yourself at how many you have been willing to throw out? You wonder how you could have held onto that old suit or dress for so long? It's the same with our diaries at work. We meet people who regularly attend meetings while privately admitting they are not really needed. How often do we deliberately seek out waste? There are direct parallels between this and getting momentum going. What you cut here, you gain elsewhere.

Cut the crap!

No one has done more to put this principle into practise than Julian Richer, founder of the hi-fi chain Richer Sounds. His London Bridge store is in the Guinness Book of Records as the 'highest annual sales per unit area' in the world. Not only is Richer brilliant at squeezing the most out of every available inch of retail space, he has institutionalised the removal of momentum barriers with a 'Cut the Crap Committee'.

The committee meets once a month and has been given free rein to remove any bureaucratic barriers that offer no tangible benefit to the company. As Julian says: 'Most companies just keep adding new systems. They never go through and clear out the obsolete ones.'

Do you know the type of project review meetings where the big boss is present and a cast of thousands lines up to present? You could say that these types of meetings are merely an exercise in control. You could be more charitable and say that it is good training for more junior people. Whatever. If you are serious about getting creative at work you have to take a sharp knife and conduct some major surgery on your meetings.

The kind of surgery we advocate is to reorganise radically how meetings work, and to label clearly what sort of meeting it is. The effect of labelling is to send clear signals to staff about how to behave. Below are five types of meeting we use when in the ER world. The aim is to cut the time we spend in meetings, freeing up plenty of time to spend in the greenhouse. We dare you to try them!

i · 'Information only' meetings

We have a company-wide meeting every month called the Big Meeting. We've now made this meeting 'information only'. We realised that trying to discuss things in such a big group just wasn't working and was taking forever. The result? Most people seem happy about it. They know their time is being respected. The loss of debate is worth the time saved. If people want to argue a point then they do so informally outside the meeting.

ii · 'Decisions only' meetings

We have smaller teams attend these meetings, where the only responses allowed are 'yes' or 'no'. The effect has been much more interest in the agenda beforehand – 'What are we being asked to agree to?' More conversations occur between participants before each 'decisions only' meeting.

iii · 'Stand up' meetings

Borrowed from the court of Queen Victoria, 'stand up' meetings cut down time spent dramatically. These meetings do not allow people to get comfortable in their chairs, enquire about each other's families, or talk about last night's game. This doesn't mean they are entirely devoid of human niceties. It's just that standing up sends clear messages that we mean business here. OK!

iv · 'Decide at the beginning' meetings

Participants agree to make all the decisions first without discussion. They simply vote 'yes' or 'no' to each item on the agenda. What is effectively happening here is that they are making the decisions real, then stepping back to see how they feel about the decisions already made. More often than not people feel good about the decisions and only feel the need to go back and discuss maybe one or two. Unnecessary small talk has been cut out and only real issues come to the fore. The reason some seemingly innocuous points get the life debated out of them in traditional meetings is more to do with defensive reactions than the issues themselves.

v · 'Rattle and roll' meetings

The insight behind this kind of meeting is that of ten agenda items only a small number are substantial. So in 'rattle and roll' meetings we rattle through the eight or so less contentious points first – we do this at speed. We all feel good, we've made progress and can settle down to discuss properly the remaining more weighty issues

Finally, as an antidote to the evils of bar coding time, we advocate 'hot house havens'. This involves stepping out of the usual work environment altogether and taking the team away from any distractions. Surprisingly, even though there is nothing new about the idea of getting out of the office and giving uninterrupted focus to your project, we find few companies do it well.

Not another awayday

Awaydays are the wrong tool for innovation for two reasons. First, they are too short. Just a single day out of the office with a packed agenda starts to feel like bar coding on a macro scale. There is simply too much to do. Creative time cannot be packed with agenda items. Too much pre-planning leaves no room to follow an idea and see where it leads you. It is amazing how much an innovation team can achieve working in an isolated cottage in the country for two or three days. Given a big enough chunk of time you soon exhaust your agenda and this is when the magic begins. 'Agendaless conversation', especially out of the office, is guaranteed to provoke creativity. Once the agenda is exhausted and you have cleared your head, then the really new creative stuff comes out. That's when the team enters an area of creativity that is much more likely to be competitive. This is just not possible if you bar code time. The second shortcoming of awaydays is that the same office environment sneaks in. Often awaydays have so many trappings of the office that there is little to distinguish them. The same people are present, information is presented in the same way, the same hierarchies exist and laptops and mobile phones are indispensable. For some companies the awayday venue is used so frequently that it feels like an office!

We advocate taking a project team well away from the office for an extended period of time to work solidly on one task. We call it hot housing and there are three tricks.

i · Plan it in advance

It's hard to countenance taking three days out of the office. The solution is to take a good look at your innovation projects. Which ones do you really want to achieve? Block out between three and five days of solid diary time for you and your team. You will find that it may not be possible for six months. But do it anyway. Signal to them how important it is to you and stick to your guns.

ii · Plan in freshness

Plan how you will run the session. Think about stimulus; think about the 4Rs. Bring along some different people to shake things up. Make sure to bring great food and wine.

iii · Make it isolated

Most of us don't get much isolation and when we do it's great. Hot housing does not include mobile phones, faxes or secret early morning office meetings. Ban them.

Summary

Children at play have an intensity and happy spontaneity. They have to be almost prised away from what they're doing and can't wait to get back to it. That's momentum.

In a business context, momentum is the management of energy. Think of it as an unrelenting energy. You can spot a team with momentum a mile off – team members buzz with energy and excitement.

Momentum is contagious, but so is inertia. Momentum breeds high corporate self-esteem and makes people feel that anything is possible. Companies lacking momentum create a culture that is self-defeating.

Creating a crisis is a short-term strategy for increasing momentum. Long-term solutions involve aligning of personal goals and motivations.

To reduce barriers to momentum: cut down the number of projects by learning to say 'no'; cut out waste, especially pointless meetings, bar coding and dull awaydays in boring hotel rooms.

signalling

You're driving and you decide to change lanes. What do you do? Look, then signal. Why? Because other drivers can't read your mind. If you make a sudden move you're probably history. It's the same with creativity at work. Unless you can let people know clearly what you're up to, what your needs are and how they can help you, your ideas will die.

Is this you?

◆ **Your meetings are a complete waste of time. People seem to be at cross purposes; some want to loosen up a bit and kick ideas around, and others just want to know what decisions you're going to make. Why are you wasting your life in such meetings, you wonder? And not for the first time.**

◆ **You find yourself disappointed after you've introduced an idea to your boss and got nothing back but reasons why it won't work.**

◆ **You get frustrated that the people around you are not receptive to your ideas, always pulling them apart.**

◆ **You wish your colleagues would learn to lighten up a bit, stop being so rational for five minutes and go with the flow of an idea.**

◆ **There are times when you wish your team would stop with the ideas and start with the action.**

Where does signalling fit?

We've explored the first four behaviours of creative people: freshness, greenhousing, realness and momentum. Now we want to talk about two different sorts of behaviour – signalling and courage. Think of these as 'enablers'. They support the first four behaviours. They are the essential driving skills needed to facilitate creativity at work. If the creative process were a car, then the first three habits would be the gears. Momentum would be the throttle, which propels the process forward. Signalling involves using your indicators to avoid a pile-up. Courage, our final creative behaviour, is the spirit of adventure – the willingness to venture out in the first place.

What is signalling?

In a nutshell, signalling is how you let a recipient of information know what state to be in when they receive your information. Do you want them to judge your idea or help you build it into a better idea?

Signalling is common sense and we do it a lot of the time. But at work few of us are taught to signal effectively, especially at the times we want to be creative.

Signalling helps us navigate between a creative, judgement-free world, and a business analysis world. It stops us crashing through our working lives mindlessly mixing the two.

Signalling saves time. It helps us decode how to be at work. If it's made clear that we will spend two hours developing alternative ideas, then two hours judging them, there is little doubt about how to be in both parts of the meeting. Unfortunately many of us waste time trying to understand what our colleagues want from us – are they looking for critical evaluation or partners in a creative journey?

Signalling helps us navigate between two worlds at work

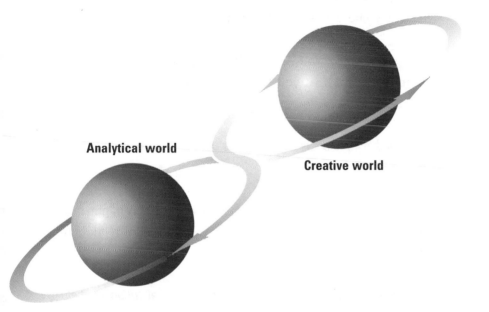

Analytical world

Creative world

The theory is simple but, believe us, signalling takes a lot of practise. However, once mastered, setting clear expectations about how you want your ideas dealt with can transform your ability to be creative with others. If greater creativity at work is your goal then signalling behaviour is not an option, it's a must. It genuinely engages and aligns a team around all the creative behaviours, making the creative process explicit and legitimate; and it drives individuals to make conscious decisions about how they want to work. Signalling puts you in the driving seat of creativity – it's great fun!

Deconstructing signalling

Signalling is a behaviour with three distinct stages.

It may only take four or five seconds to give a signal but a lot happens in that time! Imagine that you have an idea and want to share it with a colleague. The interaction might go like this:

'Jack, I think our project is stuck and I've got this radical idea about what we could do. Here goes…'

The intention is to help the project but the approach might make Jack unwilling to take up the offer. The conversation might work better if it went something like this:

'Jack, I think our project is stuck, and I've got an idea about how to help it, but I really need your help. The idea's a bit off-the-wall, so I need you to work on it with me. Is now a good time to talk it through or should we talk about it later when you're not so busy; maybe on the way to the station?'

No prizes for guessing which conversation has the best signalling!

In the second example the signaller did three things:

1. They were aware that the project was getting stuck and some creative thinking was needed to get out of their river of thinking. Maybe this was obvious, or maybe their intuition told them so. Whatever, the creative antennae were tingling – now is the time to do something different, they say!

2. The signaller decides to act. They are not drifting along with the conversation, they have decided to intervene, control and direct the process.

3. Finally, they signal. In this case a specific proposal is made. It's friendly and straightforward. Jack can either accept or say he is genuinely busy right now without feeling he has let his colleague down. He can be honest about being in business mode and not able to listen to the idea without being judgemental. The approach laid the groundwork for another meeting in the future when Jack would be aware of how the signaller wanted him to be – 'Let's talk on the way to the station.'

This is the basis of great signalling:

Tune In + Choose to Act + Propose a Response

If this formula seems overly mechanical to you there is another way of understanding signalling. We call it a 'running commentary' – you may know people who do this already.

One of the most important aspects of signalling is that it prompts you to monitor exactly what thinking style you're in – and adjust accordingly. One common observation about ?What*If*!ers from our clients is that we seem to talk as we think rather than after we have thought.

It can sometimes sound like stream of consciousness and at times it can be very unnerving to newcomers! In traditional companies, a lot of what is being thought is left unsaid, particularly as most business people seem to value making what they say sound as if it's been 'thought through' before they speak.

The divergence between what's being said and what's going on inside our heads at work is now so recognisable that cartoonists like Scott Adams (Dilbert) and others are making a living from it. They have tuned into the comic potential of what doesn't get said in business. It's like a parallel universe that exists silently alongside professional (our least favourite business word) talk at work.

Signalling may be re-expressed as a running commentary on your own thoughts. Not just what the thoughts are themselves, i.e. 'My idea is X', but what you're thinking and feeling around each idea. Here are a couple of classics...

'I'm not sure where this idea is headed, but here goes...'
(I'm going to give you stream of consciousness here and I don't even know where it's going to end up myself, so please help me.)

'This isn't a build on what you just said...'
(I'm not in creative mode, I may analyse the idea.)

If you take the last piece of self-commentary, it could easily be followed by a change of course mid-stream. So it might sound like this...

'This isn't a build on what you just said...but if I did force myself to build, then my idea is...'

What you would be hearing in this example is someone catching themselves in mid-thought. They had engaged the analytical side of their brain (as we habitually do) and course-corrected in the same stream of thought because they realised they had stopped being creative when they wished to continue.

There is a very real difference between thinking something and saying it. Every day we are bombarded by a stream of unexpressed thoughts, the accuracy and usefulness of which we rarely bother to check. The act of expressing how your thoughts are developing exposes them to your attention in a different way. You 'wake up' to what you say and remain largely unconscious of what you think. Get into the habit of expressing your thought patterns and you'll be able to navigate successfully and consciously between the creative and the ER world.

Practical signalling

1 · Signalling to seize the creative opportunity

Creative opportunities come your way like a bolt from the blue. You're not prepared for the comment your colleague has just made, your creative antennae fail to tune in, you forget to catch yourself and revert to analysis. The idea is crushed and the opportunity lost, perhaps forever.

How to manage our own creative state and that of our colleagues in the whirlwind of a normal day is a huge creative challenge. Often it's not really clear whether the moment requires creativity or not. How do we negotiate our way through these different creative states?

Imagine a half-day meeting in the board room to review next year's plan. There is a cast of thousands but not all are contributing. Each department has 20 minutes to present their plan. Most of the questions interrupting each presentation are coming from a couple of senior managers. Something isn't working.

'What is the yield on your investment in this new idea?' barks one manager. 'Why don't we link these new ideas with all our other developments?' suggests the other.

The presenter attempting to answer each question stumbles, he is not enjoying the meeting. When it's your turn to present, you summon up all your signalling skills:

'Before I start my presentation, I just want to say that I have some facts for you about next year and I want to review some of our new ideas. I'll do the facts first and you can ask me questions, and then I'll outline the new ideas. Many of these are at an early stage of development so what I really need from you are builds on how to improve each. Maybe we could even continue the conversation in the bar afterwards? Is that OK?'

What is happening here is that the people in the meeting have been given little clear guidance or direction – is it a creative meeting or is it an ER-style decision-making meeting? No matter how skilled the Chairperson, this question is often hard to answer. Some meetings, brainstorms for instance, are easy to signal as idea nurturing and judgement-free zones. But other meetings such as the one in our example are more complex, containing a mix of information requiring one minute, a nurturing response and the clinical skills of the ER. This situation is precisely when clear signalling is needed.

Let's deconstruct the approach of our signalling god in the story above.

First he noticed something was going wrong – a state of creativity was needed but if things continued the way they were, it just wasn't going to happen. His creative antennae started tingling, sending messages to his 'Creativity Mission Control'. Our hero was fully tuning in to the process of the meeting.

Next he decided to act. He'd have to break the pattern of the meeting with a proposal. So he broke his information up into chunks, explaining what he wanted.

Finally he asked (not demanded) for the response to be given in the way that he wanted. Once his audience agreed to his plan they were bound to build rather than criticise.

He tuned in + chose to act + proposed a response

This simple formula works well for meetings like this where you realise creativity is called for. It also works in the corridor! You bump into your boss in the corridor or lift, you are bursting to tell them about a new idea of yours:

'I've got this idea that just won't go away – I've got a hunch you won't agree with it but I'd really like you to go with it for a while – can you do that?'

Maybe your boss is not in the mood to hear you right now:

'I'd love to but I have a meeting – why don't we take a walk at lunchtime and discuss it?'

Or maybe your boss is in the mood:

'OK, I get what you're saying – I'll go with it – let's grab a coffee see where we can take it.'

Signalling saves the day!

Sometimes you're asked for your opinion out of the blue. The phone rings:

'Jane, it's Tom here, what do you think of my new idea?'

But hang on, your creative antennae are tingling. Are you really being asked for a judgement or for help to make the idea better? The signals are not clear, so having chosen to act you propose a response:

'Tom, can I just check with you; are you asking me to give some analysis about your idea, or do you want me to brainstorm it with you to improve it, or find alternatives?'

Remember signalling works both ways – you can send a signal to spice up creative intercourse or ask for a signal.

2 · Developing a signalling language

Use of a running commentary is the first step to moving more flexibly between a creative and analytical world within a conversation. It makes signalling a daily habit. It will allow your meetings and conversations to develop more fluidly, allowing you almost seamlessly to get creative and then reach decisions based on that creativity. It speeds things up. It feels more dynamic – and it's great fun.

There are two key skills required for signalling behaviour. First, you need to be more aware of what and how you're thinking (and feeling). Second, you need to have a language for it so that you can communicate what you notice. (As we have said, this communication is aimed at yourself as much as others!) You will have noticed how we have invented new language to help navigate between the business world and creative world. This book is peppered with verbal creative behaviour and we make no excuse for it as we know it to work. But beware, it's not all plain sailing. There does seem to be an instinctive human reaction against new vocabularies. Look at how the fields of, say, IT or psychotherapy have developed in the last ten years. You can probably remember a certain amount of ridicule aimed at these new concepts when they first started creeping into everyday speech. If you can't you're probably in denial! Sorry, but notice how that term has found its way into common usage.

The same will happen with creativity. Our clients often find the language of creative interaction uncomfortable. But eventually it becomes part accepted, part ridiculed and part tailored by each company we work with. We see this as a really healthy development. It shows the company personalising a language and adopting it as its own.

How do you feel about introducing a language of creativity into your business?

3 · Signalling a creative journey

The previous section explored creativity at its most opportunistic. Thankfully most of us have more time to plan a 'creative journey' – but we're often unaware of the importance of signalling to get the most out of it.

Let's take three examples of activities which would benefit from creativity; brainstorms, culture change programmes and annual planning processes. How does signalling work in each?

Brainstorms

You've gathered your team together off-site for a brainstorm. The key skill your facilitator needs is to tune in to the 'status' of ideas within the creative process. You may remember from the greenhousing chapter how ideas have a life span themselves – starting small and simple and growing over time as people build and conceptualise.

An important part of the facilitator's job is to set the mood for the day, to help brainstorm participants acclimatise to their new judgement-free world. But then the job gets more subtle. An experienced creative facilitator tunes into the relative health of an idea, its uniqueness and its fit with the objectives of the business, and guides the conversation using the appropriate signals.

Too often in creative sessions, people move on to the next idea before they have fully developed the idea that's on the table. Participants revel in the free-flow of thought and enthusiastically offer their next idea without trying to build on the previous contribution. This is undisciplined and signal-free creativity. At the end of such sessions, the group or team is often left with a long list of ideas that have little or no practical use. This is because they are not fully developed. In fact there was little point in the group coming together – they could just as easily have downloaded their thoughts via e-mail to the facilitator.

Far better to come away from a brainstorm with a few well-built ideas than a whole series of starting platforms which need further work. The facilitator uses signals to direct the creative energy of the team towards building on the idea that has been offered.

Key signals from the facilitator at this stage could be:
- *'Let's just stick with this idea – how can we make it better?'*
- *'I want us all to push on this – even though we may all feel exhausted.'*
- *'What do we like about this idea?'*

The skill of the facilitator is knowing what is most appropriate to the flow of creative thought. In common practise, creative sessions suffer from too much lateral movement (coverage) and not enough vertical movement (building).

Culture change

Leaders of organisations wanting to change the way business is done are engaging on an intensely creative journey. They need to give clear signals about how to be in each stage of the process – is it OK to be creative or should we be getting on and making things happen?

Here are a couple of examples of how a leader has successfully signalled to create real cultural change.

Working from home

When The Container Store, the Dallas-based home storage solution store, launched its Houston store it met with unprecedented success. They had never experienced sales of such magnitude. But while talking with the Houston store manager about what her number one priority ought to be when managing her staff, Kip Tindell, President and CEO of The Container Store realised he needed to distil a few philosophies to communicate how the business should run as it grew.

So he flew to Houston where he gathered his staff together at Amy's house to share her heartfelt philosophies on how The Container Store did business. This was not a meeting that would work in the office. Several years later the corporate values developed from that off-site session were responsible for helping The Container Store win not just once but twice the award 'Best Company In America To Work For'. The 'meeting at Amy's house' is still famous at The Container Store and is living testimony to the importance of signalling ' we're going to get creative now'.

Pause for thought

When Curt Carlson joined SRI International (formerly Stanford Research Institute) as CEO in 1998, he got his 1200-strong team of research scientists involved in developing a new project development process. Rather than tell people what the new process was, he signalled that the organisation was in a creative consultative stage and that there was an 18-month window for the team to share their vision about how the new development process could be. Today SRI's development process is famous in Silicon Valley and beyond. But, most crucially, it is owned by everybody at SRI International.

Planning processes

We see mixed evidence of leaders managing the creative state of their organisations. When will annual planning processes be clearly signalled?

For example:

'Between April and July we'll explore our options by getting fresh stimulus, nurturing ideas and making them real – then in August and September the creativity stops as we look at the business plans and numbers. That's when we'll really shake down our ideas. In October we decide.'

OK, every year might be a little too much creativity for most organisations but we hope you get the picture. Are you tuned into the need for creativity in your organisation, do you know how to signal the moves between 'exploring options' and 'making a decision' clearly?

4 Signalling to sustain creativity

A commonly shared characteristic of creative companies is their ability to signal using their environment. These signals become permanent ways of communicating to employees that creativity is important. These signals symbolise the fact that creativity is alive and well in the organisation and work is not all about 'hard' work – they give permission to play.

Here are four examples. What ideas do they give you?

The kitchen at Asda

The Asda retail business recently acquired by Wal-Mart is one of the 'big four' British retailers. In the early 1990s, a stagnant business was reinvigorated by their charismatic new leader, Archie Norman. A characteristic of his style was the clear signalling to staff about how they were expected to behave. A kitchen was built slap-bang in the middle of the marketing department. The signal was clear: don't forget we are a food business. The result of this and other initiatives at Asda was sheer magic, as anyone who visits the company will tell you. You know it is a business that cares about releasing creative potential.

Meetings rooms at HHCL

This leading UK advertising agency pioneered the use of space in their London office to signal the importance of creative behaviours – stand up meeting rooms for quick decisions; a double row of desks close to the entrance to force people to bump into each other.

The campus at Microsoft

Microsoft call their offices in Seattle a 'campus' not an HQ. The site is named and built along the lines of a university and provides far more than just office facilities. The signal is clear. We're not just another business. We value creativity and the nurturing of ideas.

The gallery at Southwest Airlines

The walls of SWA's HQ at Love Field in Dallas are covered with pictures of employees enjoying their lives outside of work. It's a clear signal that the company values their people. The signal shouts: 'Bring your whole personality to work — we want all of you here!'

In each of the signalling stories above someone somewhere tuned in to the fact that their organisation was lacking creativity. They decided to act and developed clear signals about how their people should 'be'.

Summary

Signalling is common sense and extremely valuable.

Signalling tells others how you want them to react to your idea – build it or find the holes in it.

Signalling allows you to navigate between a creative non-judgemental world and a harsher-to-ideas world of yield expectation, risk reduction, etc.

It's a behaviour that gives you power in the creative process.

Without signalling you can never effectively greenhouse an idea.

Signalling takes five seconds or less to do but years of practise to do well.

Within those five seconds three things need to happen:

Tune In, Choose to Act and Propose a Response.

courage

At this moment, as you read these words, somewhere in the world, there is a business meeting where the most amazing idea has come to someone. It started as a crazy thought but as the meeting progressed it got stronger and stronger. But that person remains silent and the idea is lost forever.

Is this you?

- **You regularly walk out of meetings thinking of something you wish you'd said.**

- **You rarely feel butterflies in your stomach anymore.**

- **You pride yourself on being a careful decision-maker: you always weigh up the pros and cons before making your mind up.**

- **You sometimes wonder if this is what you were really sent here to do.**

- **You have few strongly held convictions about your job.**

- **If you ignored your own prospects for promotion and acted on your instinct, you'd start making very different decisions.**

Stand up and be counted

Put your head above the parapet, seize the day, put your cock on the block...

When you find a subject so rich in metaphor as this, there must be lots to learn. But given its obvious importance to business success, we are intrigued by how little the subject of courage or bravery at work is talked about, written about or taught. There is a lot of material on the subject of risk avoidance, risk analysis and risk management. Of course these are important issues, but to spend so much effort thinking about risk management and so little, if any, on the positive topic of courage, appears to us plain wrong. It's like going in to a bookstore to buy *The Joy of Sex* and being told there's nothing on the subject, but 20 different books on reducing impotence! We believe that now is the time for intensely personal issues such as courage to come off the self-help shelves and right into the business section. To not engage with the real meaning and workplace interpretation of courage means creativity at work will always remain a dream.

But what is courage in business? We don't have all the answers, but we've tried to make a start. We focus on the paradoxical nature of bravery. Why is it we so admire it in others but find it hard to be brave ourselves? Why do those who are brave rarely consider themselves to be? We also look at the barriers to courage and explore how can we start to overcome them. We've attempted to give you practical tools and yet we're well aware that this subject is a lifelong journey of learning. Our aim is to switch a light on for you, to illuminate the link between courage and creativity and stimulate some searching questions.

"It is not because things are difficult that we do not dare; it is because we do not dare that things are difficult."
SENECA

We use the words courage and bravery more or less interchangeably.

Courage and creativity

There is something about the concept of courage. It fascinates and enthrals us. People who possess it in business carry a talismanic power. The Bransons, Gates, Jobs and Roddicks of this world inspire us with their ability to jump in with both feet and do what many of us would only dream of doing, seemingly disregarding the risks. Most of us would intuitively accept that courage is one of the magical ingredients in the make-up of great business leaders and great businesses. Often it is a moment of bravery, a mould-breaking step, that becomes the landmark of a celebrated business career, or the turnaround point for emerging and established businesses alike. Think of your own favourite success stories. Did any of your heroes do what they did without courage? Highly unlikely. Think again and notice if that act was also driven by an innovative approach at some level. The answer will nearly always be 'yes'. We're not saying that courage is a guarantee of success (for every millionaire IT entrepreneur there must be many bankrupt dot coms), more that acting without bravery is the best way to prevent success.

Creativity and courage have long been soul mates. Even at the most simple level, a new idea represents a new connection, something that hasn't been put together before. It requires the creative person to stand up and dare to be different.

Persuading colleagues to try fresh new stimulus is never easy. Making space outside the ER world to search for alternatives is never guaranteed success. Making ideas real always requires extra effort (remember the 400-pound Bengal tiger?). Galvanising a team to change priorities and generate new momentum is always harder than 'business as usual'. Tuning in and signalling how you want your ideas dealt with will feel plain weird to begin with.

"There is a microscopically fine line between being brilliantly creative and acting like the most gigantic idiot on earth. So what the hell, leap!"
CYNTHIA HEIMEL

So having the guts to get on and make a difference is the subtext to this whole book. If you practise our creative behaviours you'll find yourself going against the flow of what has gone before. That's when you know you can really make a difference.

What is courage?

The original meaning of the word 'courage' is 'to speak your mind with all your heart'. There is something that unites the courageous, some quality of self. The origins and anatomy of courage are profoundly intimate. They are about being true to yourself. Early in his career, Formula 1 Grand Prix Champion Nigel Mansell sold everything he owned, even mortgaged his house to raise money to race. He didn't set out to be brave, he just did what he truly believed in. Brave people often disclaim their act with the terms, 'I had no choice' or 'I just set out to do what I knew I had to do.' Courage is the label of the onlooker but not the intention of the principal involved.

This is a crucial point. Courage is not an innate quality, something you've got or you haven't. Neither is courage an irresistible impulse over which you have no control. By getting under the skin of what courage really means we believe you can, with practise, develop your courage as a powerful creative behaviour. If courage is to 'speak your mind with all your heart', then knowing what's in your heart is what matters. Or to put it another way, having the courage of your convictions means you need to be convicted in the first place – to believe strongly enough in something to make a stand. Here we get to the key point about courage and creativity at work – the language and environment of traditional business is still not designed to open our hearts and take intuition seriously. 'I believe' is less acceptable than 'I know'.

At work, many of us subconsciously prefer not to push too hard. We hold back from truly letting go and releasing our whole unique selves into the creative process. We monitor the relative acceptability of our ideas and hold back the more off-the-wall thoughts in fear of judgement. It takes real courage to let the connections of the mind pour forth. It is very self-exposing; yet this is the very essence of creativity.

Rabbit in the headlights...

Get a small group of colleagues standing together in a circle and place an object, any object, in the middle. The purpose of the game is to mime a use for the object until someone gets it. So an object like a video cassette becomes a surfboard, an axe, a mobile phone, etc. Don't force people to play; let them step forwards when they feel comfortable. What you will discover is that some people step forward more readily than others. The ones who hold back are caught in the headlight of their fears. Yet even the ones who step forward will produce mimes that are typically very obvious, taking just a split second to guess. They, in turn, are caught in the fear of miming in full view with nobody getting it. Lead a discussion with the group and you will probably find that most people thought of something much more obtuse and off-the-wall but didn't dare do it. Now go back to the game. Change the rules. Ask people to step into the middle without a thought of what they are going to do – to pick up the object and just go with it. This requires true spontaneous creativity – a free-flow of connection. The game will move a lot slower than before, as people struggle to let go of their need to plan, to quickly assess the 'suitability' of an idea before exposing it to the world.

This simple game is illustrative of how creativity happens in the business world. True creativity requires us to be our true selves, to expose our true selves, and for many of us it is much easier to play safe, to offer safe ideas that we believe will be accepted. This leads to creativity of sorts, to incrementalism. No bad thing in itself, but like grape juice to the rich claret of true innovation.

Courage is vital to the creative process, then, because it enables those individuals to offer the full power of their minds, their spontaneous creative connection-making, without self-censoring to mediocre acceptability. Again, this is the quality of being true to yourself, of stating what you are capable of, and having the personal integrity to know that this self-expression is what really matters most, not the judgement of others. It is this strength of self that facilitates the other key aspect of creativity, the ability to let go of one's own view of the world and go with the flow of someone else's thinking (the 'suspend judgement' part of SUN).

It seems obvious that we are much more likely to produce a new connection if we open up to a new way of thinking. Often, it involves an approach from someone else that at first impression to us seems 'wrong' or 'wasteful', or just different (outside our own 'ideas bandwidth'). This combination of being true to yourself and yet at the same time having the humility to let go of your own view may seem at first contradictory. This is the real skill of creative people. Those who lack this ability can react like a wounded cat and pounce on your idea. The most defensive people are invariably those who are least sure of themselves – that is why they react so quickly to make themselves look strong.

Creativity, in summary, is an act which is intimately related to courage, and consequently to our own personal strength, our ability to be who we are, true to ourselves.

> *"All the significant battles are waged within the self."*
>
> SHELDON KOPP

Try for yourself

Ask several entrepreneurs whom you believe to have shown great bravery whether they consider themselves to be unusually brave. Very few of them will answer 'yes'. More often they will simply describe a situation where they felt they had no choice but to act as they did. This is certainly true for us at ?What *If!* When we first left our comfortable corporate jobs for a minimal wage and a single Apple Mac, people thought we were showing extraordinary bravery. They kept slapping us on the back and saying, 'Good luck, I wish I had your balls!' It wasn't like that for us. We simply had to live our dreams. We weren't being brave, we simply felt we had no choice.

In our view bravery is entirely relative. Its source lies deep within ourselves, not by comparison with others. For this reason, bravery is accessible to all. It is the habit of those who know who they are and remain true to that vision.

"People cannot discover new oceans until they have the courage to lose sight of the shore."

ANON

Practical steps

Imagine you are in a planning meeting for next year. Your mind has just produced this crazy but intriguing and creative connection – should you say anything? What will the response be? It's decision time.

Let's dig deep into the structure of such a decision and explore the factors that will help determine the outcome. Imagine yourself in the situation above, but now it's in a movie, and the movie is employing one of those freeze-frame devices where everybody else stops. You come out of your body, and discuss, Woody Allen-style, the pros and cons of the action you might take. In our version of the film, there are five practical steps which you can take and, like Woody, we're going to present them before you in all their introspective glory.

1 · Show your struggle

All of us are held back by our fears. They are the self-limiting beliefs which constrain the release of our creative potential. For most of us, they were learnt before we were eight years old, yet they live on, real as ever, whether they are relevant now or not.

Take the planning meeting example. What would Woody say?

'You gotta be joking, you can't say that, they'll think you're crazy, that idea is the product of a sick mind. Before the brainstorm is through the group will have reported to the boss and there'll be a brown envelope waiting on your desk. You've gotta wife and kids to support – my God! Let's get the hell out of here!'

We're exaggerating to make the point, but to some extent we are all trapped like this in the headlight of our fears. Fear of failure, of looking stupid; fear of not being good enough, smart enough, creative enough. All these lead to that all-encompassing human fear – rejection. Rejection from the group (our colleagues), from the family. In short, our fears play a huge part in preventing us from performing to our true creative potential. They strangle the brave idea before it sees the light of day.

Perhaps you recognise yourself in this or perhaps you don't. If you're in the latter category, congratulations, but take a minute to consider others – remember that creativity is almost always enhanced as a group activity. Being aware of the fears of others is just as important as connecting with your own.

Somehow a fear left unspoken grows in the mind. The great thing is there's a very simple antidote. Don't be afraid to show your struggle. If you're stuck, really struggling with that crazy seedling idea that just won't go away then show your colleagues your struggle.

Using our signalling skills it goes like this:

'I'm not sure whether I should say this or not I'm really stuck but rather than bottle it up I'm just gonna let it all out. Is that OK?'

Don't be afraid to show the pain of your struggle and indecision. Perhaps the person above delivered this line with a face contorted by the strain of their struggle. The point is that nobody wants to work with smartass know-it-alls. When faced with another's 'stuckness', when they show us fuzzy undeveloped ideas, and more than that they recognise them as unfinished, it's hard not to want to help. People who publicly acknowledge their own creative struggle like this have real courage. The possibility of ridicule, the clever put-down, is far outweighed by the connection and goodwill the struggle creates between a committed team.

> ## *"The greatest mistake you can make in life is to be continually fearing you will make one."*
> ALBERT G. HUBBARD

When OK isn't OK

Here's an example of real courage from one of the team at ?What *If!*

'A colleague asked me to read a proposal that they were about to send to a client. They had worked over their holidays on it and really wanted to be told it was fine, with perhaps a couple of minor tweaks. As we talked it through, it became clear that, whilst it was basically fine, there was another way of writing it that could be stronger, but it would mean starting all over again. The timid advice would be, "Use your own judgement, you might be able to tweak it, it's probably OK." The brave advice is, "I'm afraid you'll have to redo it if you want it to be better."'

If you've ever had people report to you you'll be familiar with work which is clearly not up to scratch. That's easy to sort out. What's hard is when the people are OK and their work is OK but not special or magical. That's when real courage is needed. Whenever you let things ride that are OK (because changing them would be difficult for them and would make you personally unpopular), you'll always regret it later. Fudging the issues, and walking away from difficult discussions makes you unpopular far more effectively than being direct and honest.

This is not about the courage of a maverick entrepreneur who owned their own company. And it's not about people and life-changing acts of bravery (moving abroad, leaving your partner, etc.). Very often what calls for courage is the fact that you don't face a stark choice between right or wrong but basically OK and potentially (but not definitely) better.

2 · Always stretch your Comfort Zone

Courage is entirely relative – what is brave to you is an everyday act to someone else and vice versa. The important thing is that you take the time to understand what stretches you. All of us have our own particular fears that hold us back. If you want to break through this, you must start with self-awareness. We do this using a simple model.

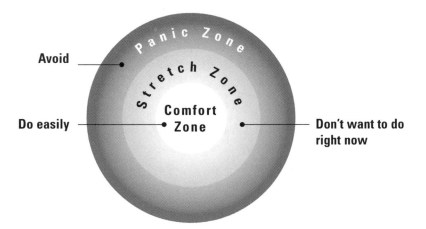

The Comfort Zone represents what we do most days in our lives without a second thought. The Stretch Zone is our area of personal development. We have to face one of our fears to do it. The Panic Zone represents things we just don't want to do. We find many ways of avoiding this zone.

How does this relate to you and creativity? Where would you plot some of the creative behaviours on this diagram? If you've read this far in the book you must be pretty interested in what we have said about creativity (either that or you are in prison or on a very long cruise). You must be able to recall some of the freshness, greenhousing or realness actions you've contemplated taking. Where do you place them on the diagram? If some of them aren't in the Stretch Zone then you're either kidding yourself or you're not committed enough to developing your creative behaviour.

3 · Get convicted

Let's go back to the meeting above where you kept quiet. You leave the meeting having said nothing, just like everybody else. 'No big deal,' you tell yourself at first, but the little voice just won't go away. 'You had something to offer, you could have made a real difference,' it says. With regret you admit, 'I should really have said something.' What we are doing in our heads is rehearsing the scene. The problem is that the scene has passed. It's too late for a rehearsal. Rehearsals work before the event. In general, very few of us are in the habit of visioning how we want to be, running things through our head, describing a clear picture of how things could be. Without this picture there's no conviction of how great things could be, so in rush the fears, and out pops the pragmatist! A mediocre idea is born.

A basic practical creative behaviour is to start each future focused meeting with a few minutes from everyone visualising what their idea of amazing success is. Make it real.

'Good morning everybody. Before we start let's take a couple of minutes to imagine that it is 5.30pm and we are walking out of the door. We're slapping each other on the back feeling incredibly excited by the ideas we've had. We're all buzzing with a sense of possibilities. Let's hear from each of you what types of things we have explored in the meeting.'

> **"Avoiding danger is no safer in the long run than outright exposure. Life is either a daring adventure, or nothing."**
>
> HELEN KELLER

What's important here is that you're attaching yourself to a vision that is personally motivating. This attachment provides the crucial motivation to step beyond your Comfort Zone and through your fears. You are making courage come more easily because you are helping yourself get convicted that you can do it, that you are on the right track. Visualisation is the technique of deliberately creating a picture of success, then focusing on the benefits and rewards of our efforts. It involves focusing beyond the pain, to the gain.

Major athletes have been practicing this for years. They work on their ability to visualise success in their minds, to actually picture themselves winning. Have you ever watched a high jumper visualise every stride of their run and jump? The brain reacts to this visual image every bit as powerfully as if it were happening in real life. It has been recorded that athletes produce 'winning' hormones, just by visualising success. It's why so much of sport is referred to as a mind game; why winning the mental battle is as important as the physical and why so many sports teams and athletes have motivational coaches.

4 · Pay attention to self-commentary

The sad fact is that many people become used to not achieving their full potential at work. In fact, being who we really could be is much scarier than staying where we currently are. Not being brave becomes a habit – ingrained in us, expected from us and by us. We see this when we audit our clients' staff's hobbies and skills outside work. It is always a surprise just how creative and active many people are. Occasionally we let our hair down and show our true selves to be greeted with that painful, 'I never knew you were like that' comment. Maybe we have let ourselves become so far removed from who we really want to be that the move seems too scary. Paralysed by the scale of this change, we make no changes at all. Fear and compromise thrive in this environment. Our habits become set and we do nothing to challenge them. 'I've never challenged the boss before, so why should I start now?' We all talk to ourselves about ourselves – there is a tape that plays over and over again – a self-generated running commentary on us, by us. Sometimes it's complimentary but often not. Many people don't take care to talk to themselves positively – 'I'm not creative, why would anyone listen to me, they don't respect me...' Years of this becomes a self-fulfilling prophecy.

So pay attention to what you say. Watch out for the undermining negative snipes. Instead encourage the positive. Remember, what you focus on and talk about grows. Deepak Chopra describes this with a beautiful metaphor, that of imagining yourself 'wrapped in a cloak' made of the words you use about yourself. It's a very simple and effective creative behaviour.

> *"It is our choices, Harry, that show what we truly are, far more than our abilities."*
>
> J K ROWLING

5 · Find your friends

Everything that we are talking about here is easy to say, hard to do. The behaviour of creative courage is a real self-investment. But many organisational cultures make an already difficult terrain even more hazardous. They just don't encourage or support bravery. The challenge to senior management is not welcomed, the off-the-wall idea greeted with a sarcastic quip, the brave act grudgingly recognised, not celebrated and rewarded. In such environments, bravery is even more difficult. This lack of support from leadership, and from the company culture as a whole, is frequently cited by business people as the main barrier to bravery.

Our practical advice is not to embark on a journey of creativity alone. When Luke Skywalker set out to do battle with Darth Vader and the Evil Empire he found some friends. The Rebel Alliance, of which he became part, was a group where bravery could flourish because of a common purpose and constant sharing and support. Too often bravery is typecast as a solitary occupation.

Perhaps your reality is very different. You may not have the captain of the fastest starship in the galaxy, a princess and a seven-foot Wookie at your side, but you do need to create your own support systems. For thoughts on what you need, why not watch *Star Wars*? Who is your Jedi master training and advising you, helping you understand when to fight and when to wait? Who are your Han and Leia, constantly at your side sharing the burden and the risks, and pulling you out of the fire in times of trouble? Like the Alliance, do you have leaders who provide motivation and vision, who understand what bravery is and lead by example?

Don't get caught up in the myth of the solitary hero. It's a lot easier to be brave if you know there's someone watching out for you.

A final word

That which gets rewarded happens. We're not talking about cash rewards, we're talking about human recognition; the love and belonging we all crave. If you want brave action (and not all of you reading this book will), then promote it.

Promote it as a value in your company and talk openly about those actions that fit the value. Promote the people who display it. Look for signs of it in your recruitment procedure, for example, by asking explicitly: 'What mistakes have you learnt from most?' And don't stop at the first three prepared answers. Publicise brave success stories – look at Southwest Airlines Wall of Fame, a veritable living museum in honour of their bravehearts! Learnings not mistakes. Everyone, but especially leaders, must talk about learning.

The Learning Account

Eric Peacock is a serial entrepreneur. After working for the Hanson Group, Eric set about buying up underperforming companies and turning their fortunes around. Just one of his successes is Babygro, the infant clothing company which grew 450% in three years under Eric's stewardship, and on to a full stock market listing. One of the secrets of his success is the 'Learning Account'. All expenditure that was intended but failed to drive growth is accounted for separately in Eric's companies. The Learning Account is rigorously reviewed by senior managers for its learning value to the company, and cascaded through the organisation.

Make it clear and public that things which do not work out as planned will be openly discussed, and the learnings taken and made public. This should become an everyday part of your business, as inevitable as an annual planning meeting. If the organisation brushes its failures under the carpet and pretends they don't happen, a stigma grows and people feel less inclined to take a risk. Richer Sounds, the super-successful UK hi-fi retailer, includes a list of the company's greatest mistakes in its induction pack for new starters – you can't get much more of a clear cultural signal than that! A culture of learning is a seed-bed for acts of courage.

Summary

Creativity is by definition closely related to bravery, because it requires the creator to expose themselves to potential judgement.

Brave people do not think of themselves as brave, they are merely being true to themselves.

Courage can be life-changing but also the everyday behaviour of not being satisfied with just OK performance.

Practical steps you can take are:

◆ Show your struggle.

◆ Stretch your Comfort Zone regularly and deliberately.

◆ Get convicted – don't wait for belief to come to you but visualise how things could be.

◆ Cloak yourself in positive self-commentary.

◆ Find your friends and support each other.

a call to arms

A Call to Arms

[a call to arms]

Many organisations have realised that the world of work is changing rapidly. The important dynamics of business success are becoming increasingly related to human factors. A new management science, or perhaps more accurately art, is emerging, and for the first time the concept of managing the human mind is being taken seriously.

This book is a call to arms for those 21st century business pioneers whose intuition, perhaps business experience, has led them to the same conclusion as we have, that creativity, human beings operating at the fullness of their potential, can create that spark of difference, added value and unique-ness that holds the key to sustainable business advantage this century. In a world where organisations and individuals have access to the same information flows and data, the advantage will favour those who realise incremental innovation is not enough; that the cultivation and development of creative behaviours is the key to success in a competitive environment.

We sound a warning to all those sitting on big market shares and send a shining beam of encouragement to those with fewer res-ources. The days of relying on clever down-sizing are gone. A more positive, expan-sionist, creative surge is required; the creativity of growth, not restriction. Welcome to the 21st century, where business will be driven by the human mind as the predominant market factor, and the management of human imagination as the most prized skill.

We call to those people who see clearly that the tide of business history is turning, who see an emerging creative community, who want to shape the future. They are business people, driven by results, by the bottom line, and yet still excited at the opportunity for their businesses to grow in harmony with human development. The winning businesses of this century will be peopled by value-led, happy, balanced, emotionally engaged and motivated groups aligned to a common goal.

The creative behaviours described in this book represent a big first step for those who wish to experience what it is to be creative in a business context. For yourself, and those you lead, you should be aware it won't always be easy to operate at a creative level at work. But by making yourself change the habitual, comfortable things; letting go of the familiar world of quick judgement, creating an alternative view when time tells you to quickly move on, making things real, you will succeed. Take responsibility for your ideas, express who you are, have the strength to live that vision in spite of your fears.

Good luck. Welcome to the revolution.

Index